The Management Game

Simulated Decision Making

F. *ranklin* Warren McFarlan

James L. McKenney

John A. Seiler

Harvard University

THE MACMILLAN COMPANY
COLLIER-MACMILLAN LIMITED, LONDON

© Copyright, The Macmillan Company, 1970

First Printing

THE MACMILLAN COMPANY
866 Third Avenue, New York, New York 10022
COLLIER-MACMILLAN CANADA, LTD., TORONTO, ONTARIO

Printed in the United States of America

Preface

The Management Game is a product of the long process of gaming development at Harvard. The distant ancestor of this simulation was first created at UCLA in 1957 and has been steadily evolving ever since, most recently under the name of the HBS Management Simulation. It has been used for a wide variety of pedagogical purposes in many types of educational programs. Its applications have ranged from being used as a vehicle to permit examination of the process of forming an explicit statement of a business strategy to an application in conjunction with a course in human relations. It is being used currently in such varied settings as undergraduate business schools, graduate business schools, on-campus executive training programs, and in-company training programs.

The Simulation is copyrighted by the President and Fellows of Harvard College and we appreciate their permission to reproduce it.

As the game is an outgrowth of activities at the Harvard Business School, we are indebted to Dean George Baker and Associate Dean George Lombard for providing us the time and opportunity to develop it. Those faculty members who provided us with the advice and encouragement to undertake and modify this structure are too numerous to individually thank, but without their involvement and enthusiasm this simulation would never have been developed. Our special gratitude goes to Mrs. Patricia Glavin Colton, Mr. Elden Zigler, Miss Donna Bergmark, and Mrs. Susan Rogers for the valuable assistance they provided in the development of the programs and administrative procedures which made the simulation an operational entity. Finally, we would like to express our appreciation to our secretaries, Mrs. Nancy Hayes and Miss Rosalie Allen, for the long hours spent typing and retyping this manuscript.

F. W. M.
J. L. M.
J. A. S.

iii

Contents

Chapter 1

Introduction

The HBS Management simulation is designed to provide an experience in business decision making under uncertainty. It will involve you in the problems of developing and implementing an economic strategy in an ongoing business. You will participate in the simulation by managing a firm in conjunction with several of your classmates. This firm will compete in a consumer goods industry against several other firms manned by other classmates. There are a variety of firm structures that may be adopted depending upon the size of the total class. All forms of involvement, however, are operationally concerned with the relationship of the individual plant to the markets it serves. The first three chapters are concerned with introducing you to the operation in general, how your market functions, and the economics of your production facilities. As organizational structure is important in how you obtain funds from external sources and control internal funds, the specific forms of organization will be discussed at the introduction of the fourth chapter, which deals with finance.

The demand for the firm's products will be dependent upon their *price, quality*, and *timing* of advertising and promotion expenditures. Early in the simulation experience, you will be provided with information concerning the industry's or industries' market structure and the available resources. Based on this information you will be required to formulate a competitive strategy.

The bulk of the simulation will be given to the implementation of this strategy in the simulated environment. This implementation will include setting prices for your products, determining their quality, scheduling their production, making allocations for their promotion, and financing your firm's operations. The end product of your analysis will be a plan for a quarter of the year's operation of your firm, in the form of a decision set.

During the life of the simulation, the foregoing variables must be analyzed constantly so that appropriate modifications to your plan of action can be established as necessary.

After each set of decisions you will receive the results of your firm's operations for the quarter in the form of reports; Chapters 5, 6, and 7 explain these in detail. This information will permit you to evaluate your performance and improve your understanding of the firm's environment. The number of decision sets you will complete will be determined by your instructor.

Information Sources

A primary task in managing your firm will be the acquisition of relevant decision-making information. There are four sources of information. The first source of data is provided for you in the form of four periods of past performance and history. These data will provide background information on the firm's operations from which you can discern how the production phase functions and observe the influence of seasonality on demand.

The second source of information is contained in these instructions which explain the general range of the determinants of demand, as well as explaining how you may schedule production for your products and finance your firm's operations.

The third and most important source of information will be the quarterly reports that you will receive after *each* period of decision making. These reports will be in the same *form* as the initial history, and will give full and precise information on the firm. You will also receive general industry data describing your competitors. Data, such as your competitors' total sales revenue, prices, and financial data, which would be public knowledge in real life, will be reported accurately; however, data, such as product sales volume, product quality, and advertising and sales promotion expenditures, which would not be public knowledge, will be given only approximately.

The fourth source of information comes from available market research data that may be *purchased* as it is deemed necessary. These data may be acquired for any product you are currently selling or would like to sell.

Thus at the beginning of the simulation, relatively little information is available about the market and competition. Although the simulation's design incorporates many general characteristics of actual industries, it is not a reproduction of any specific industry. Since many distinctive aspects of each firm's individual market will be created by its actions and those of its competitors, the firm must analyze the gross data to understand its industry's characteristics in order to create and implement a successful strategy.

General approach to stimulation

After becoming familiar with the introductory materials, your firm is expected to decide on objectives and then to formulate operating policies designed to achieve these objectives. You will be able to develop more detailed and perhaps more useful operating policies or strategies as you gain more knowledge about your environment. However, one of the most effective approaches has proved to be an attempt to formulate plans early in the simulation to identify what you do not know and to quickly familiarize yourself with the data. The simulation is so designed that any number of different strategies can be successful (e.g., high volume – low price, low volume – high price). The particular objectives you adopt should be appropriate for your firm's specific competitive environment. A careful digestion of these instructions and the four quarters of historical data on the operation of your firm should provide an adequate basis to develop appropriate tentative objectives. How nearly you achieve your objectives is dependent upon how well you analyze the available information and prepare a plan of action that is consistent with your strategy. As you will note in the following instructions, fluctuating behavior will be penalized. Your success will be dependent, in large measure, not so much on what particular objectives you adopt, but rather on how well you plan ahead so that your individual moves achieve a cumulative momentum toward your objectives.

Chapter 2
Market Environment

Determinants of demand

Total demand for an industry's products is determined externally by general economic conditions and internally by industry activity.

The external influence comes from both seasonal factors and cyclical variations in general economic conditions. The firm's income statement (see Exhibit 3, p. 31) contains a seasonally adjusted business index. This business index, reflecting the gross national product, represents the general level of economic activity and not the seasonal influences present in the industry. The business index is calculated as if there is no seasonal influence in the market. An improvement of 5 percent in the business index may be offset by the normal seasonal downswing. The indices are precise for present and past periods, but the accuracy of the forecasted indices decreases as they become longer range. The normal level of economic activity is about 700. In the absence of counteracting influences such as price cuts or increased marketing expenditures, total industry demand swings upward and downward with the index. When the business index is falling, consumers are more price conscious than they are when the index is rising. Industry demand is also subject to seasonal variations, which tend to repeat themselves every four quarters. In general, seasonal influences occur with more regularity than do cyclical influences. All industries will be subjected to the same set of seasonal and business cycle variations.

The *internal* influence of industry activity is a more important determinant of total industry demand than external economic developments. The degree to which the industry as a whole exploits the market is dependent on the combined marketing expenditures of the several firms and the extent to which the needs of various consumer segments are satisfied. Potential customers differ in their sensitivities toward price, toward marketing expenditures, and toward product quality; therefore, the industry can best exploit its market by offering products that appeal to all consumer segments.

The market is segmented and the segments differ in size. All products, regardless of their marketing mix, will be sold to some degree in all market segments. However, only those products whose price, marketing outlays, product quality, and product development best match the corresponding sensitivities of a market segment will achieve a significant market share in that particular segment.

The demand for any given product of a firm is dependent upon that product's price, its quality relative to that of similarly priced products, its promotion, its advertising, its product development expenditures, and its availability for sale. The best method of identifying your competitors is to rank all products in an industry by price; those closest to your own are your keenest competitors. Products that are very close together in price will compete vigorously with one another for market share, without greatly expanding the size of their total market. There is relatively little competitive interaction between products differing widely in price.

The product number has no significance (i.e., Product 1 of one firm will not compete with other Product 1's in the industry unless their price is close).

Sales demand for your products is dependent upon your expenditures on sales promotion, advertising, and product development. Sales promotion expenditures are employed for launching a new product or repositioning an existing product that has been improved. Sales promotion expenditures are used only when you intend to change your existing product line, and they can be considered to cover the costs of special detail salesmen, special displays, and introductory dealer discounts to establish distribution for the new or changed product. Advertising expenditures, on the other hand, are of a longer term nature and are for the purpose of building brand image and awareness among the ultimate consumers. Advertising expenditures encompass both media expenditures and agency fees. Product development expenditures must be made continuously to maintain the perceived quality of an established product through improvements in product design, styling, packaging, and quality control.

Marketing activities by one industry will *in no way* affect demand in other industries, Each industry is completely separate from the other.

Marketing insights

The following information is hand-me-down experience concerning the behavior of the market, such as that obtained by a marketing executive from his predecessors when he tackles a new job. You may assume that the following information is accurate, but you should not assume that it is complete.

Number of Products

Each plant may manufacture up to three products simultaneously. A change of more than 30 percent in the price of a product from one period to the next is considered by the market to be a change of product.

Total Industry Sales

Total market size is a function of industry activity and will grow or diminish according to the plant's decisions. An example of the economic diversity that may result is a recent simulation which included two identical industries with aggregate annual sales of $16 million at the start. At the conclusion of three simulated years, one industry had annual sales of $44 million and the other had sales of $18 million. At that time the total market and an annual secular growth of 4.5 percent. The total market in any quarter was further modified by a seasonal factor representing the quarterly sales pattern of the industry.

The Five Market Segments

Sales are generated in five sectors or market segments, each of which is influenced by all previous and present marketing decisions. The five sectors are differentiated by their initial relative size and by their particular response to the determinants of demand. They represent five consumer segments. The absolute size of each sector is influenced by the economic index and the seasonal factor. This combination of influences creates the following relationships:

1. The market becomes more price sensitive in time of economic downturn.

2. After several quarters of economic upturn the market becomes increasingly price insensitive.

3. Nonprice competition will expand the market, but not as much as a price spread among competitors.

4. A sales growth may be the result of growth of sales by the industry, or acquisition of a competitor's potential sales, depending on quality improvements, marketing budgets, and price.

5. A plant can create and maintain for itself a market if it maintains an edge in the demand determinants at that price-quality range, e.g., a product with a $20 price, $10 quality, and $80,000 marketing budget would hold its market share in competition with a product of $19 price, $9 quality, and a $50,000 marketing budget.

6. Lost sales of a plant go to competitors.

These relationships can be modified rather easily prior to the start of a simulation, so that previously published descriptions of the simulation need not apply to the one in which you will participate. As an example of the characteristics of the five consumer segments *as the simulation was played in a previous year*, the following description is offered for your appraisal.

The largest segment was most influenced by price, assuming similar marketing budgets and an acceptable quality ratio. It was strongly affected by the economic index.

The next largest segment was most influenced by the price to quality ratio, with an acceptable level of product development necessary. This sector was the most seasonally dependent, but it had the greatest long-term sales stability; it did not decay easily.

The next three segments were about the same size. One was influenced most by marketing and quality. Another segment was influenced equally by quality and product development. It was fairly price insensitive, but sensitive to the economic index. The final segment was influenced most by price. This sector had no stable demand, it responded to market activity.

It should be emphasized that the five consumer segments just described are illustrative only. The nature of the consumer segments in your version of the simulation may bear no exact resemblance to them.

Determinants of Market Share

All products will be sold, to some degree, in all market segments. However, a product's market share in a particular segment may be tiny if its marketing mix is perceived as inappropriate to the tastes of consumers in that segment.

Each demand determinant of price, product development, and quality, and marketing (advertising and sales promotion) has a unique influence on the plant's market share.

*Price.** Price has the largest influence in the market and when changed causes the quickest market reaction.

A one percent downward price change may result in an increase of 2 to 5 percent in demand for a product. However, similarly priced products will tend to divide up a market within a particular price range, with little total market expansion. The full effects of a price increase are felt at once, whereas those of a decrease develop more slowly. Demand for a product price beyond $44 will not support the expense of keeping a product alive. Products priced below $4 will not bring a profitable return. All price changes have to be announced one period in advance, thereby allowing competitors to adjust their production plans in the subsequent period.

Product Quality. The quality of a product is determined by the amount of labor and material value put into the product in the manufacturing operations. Labor value is comprised of labor cost per unit in both the fabrication and assembly departments. Material value is subdivided into the cost per unit of purchased parts and the cost per unit of raw material. At a *minimum*, products must have $.60 worth of labor, of which $.40 must be fabrication and $.20 must be assembly; and $.90 work of materials of which $.60 must be raw material and $.30 must be purchased parts. The following are examples of normal products for this market.

Fabrication labor	$ .40	$ .75	$1.05	$1.40	$2.40	$ 3.60	$ 4.50
Assembly labor	.20	.40	.75	1.40	4.50	10.80	17.10
Raw Material	.60	.85	1.10	1.35	2.20	3.40	4.50
Purchased parts	$1.30	.35	.40	.45	.60	.80	1.00
Quality Total	$1.50	$2.35	$3.30	$4.60	$9.70	$18.60	$27.10

*At the beginning of each decision period, each plant will be aware of its competitor's planned prices for that period.

The market is sensitive to the relative proportion among the four labor and material components; the market accords full value to the costs of inputs within a normal range. Unusual proportions of any component are discounted by consumers, who will not accord to such products the full quality image they seemingly deserve.

A one percent change in the cost per unit for a product may result in a $\frac{1}{2}$ to 3 percent change in demand, the larger change applying especially to large markup items, and the smaller to low price, low markup items. The consumer reacts quickly to changes. The effect of downward cost changes is even more rapid than that of upward ones. Relative quality is a significant factor in calculating demand for similarly priced products. The market for high-priced products may allow a lower quality ratio than that which prevails in the lower priced products.

There are three types of marketing effort: promotion, advertising, and product development. They differ according to the time of their impact upon the market and their time influence in the market. Each has a most effective range for a given level of sales; in other words, one has to spend a certain amount to obtain any influence, and beyond a certain amount the added dollar of expenditures does not return that amount in profitable sales dollars. It is up to you to analyze the sales data to determine the limits and elasticity of the sales response to the various types of marketing expenditures.

Advertising. Advertising is the largest of the three budgets and typically will have the greatest influence of the three decisions. The effects of changes in advertising expenditures are felt fairly quickly, with downward changes taking hold more quickly than upward ones. A sudden downward shift in advertising expenditures is given an immediate unfavorable interpretation by the trade; it takes longer for consumers to react favorably to an increase in outlays. An increase in a relatively low advertising budget by 10 percent may result in an increase of as much as 6 or 8 percent in demand for a product. But a doubling of an already large budget (e.g., $700,000 per period) may result in as little as a 3 percent increase. Sales reaction to a change in the budgetary level is most noticeable in the quarter the change occurs and in the quarter following. An advertising expenditure should be budgeted each quarter. Each expenditure has a discernible effect on product sales for about four quarters after it is made. The threshold of expenditure and maximum effective range are influenced by the price and unit volume of the product. For low-priced products, a minimum of $100,000 per quarter is necessary to have a significant effect. For products over $20 that have a sales volume of under 50,000 units, $100,000 is about the upper level of expenditure. The reasonable range of advertising budget for all products is from about $.30 per unit to $8 per unit.

A firm's advertising outlays for one of its products to some extent enhances demand for its other products. (For corporations organized under alternatives B, C, D and E, these advertising expenditures do not affect the demand for the products of the corporation's other plants or divisions.)

Promotion. Promotion expenditures have a greater impact but do not stimulate demand for as long a period as do advertising budgets. Promotion outlays consist of special dealer incentives (e.g., special per-case allowances) and consumer deals (e.g., cents-off promotions and couponing), which will serve to buy a market position in the short run, but which cannot sustain distribution in the long run. Promotion has a short-term effect only, whereas advertising will support continuing normal distribution. Expenditures should precede by at least one quarter the introduction of a new product or a significant change in the old one. Product changes for which promotion expenditures would be appropriate are a price cut of greater than 5 percent, a 20 percent increase in the product development expenditure, or a 15 percent rise in product quality. The effect of a well-timed promotion expenditure is a rapid market penetration or increased sales for an established product. A well-timed promotion budget will accelerate sales growth from 24 percent to 30 percent. Promotion budgets could range typically from 30 to 70 percent of the advertising budget.

Product Development. Product development expenditures pay for styling and developing new products, improving the packaging of present products, and other normal long-term product outlays. Changes in product development are noticeable two quarters after they have been made, and they continue for eight quarters. The changes have a very long cumulative effect that is more significant in the medium- and high-priced products than in the lower priced ones. The effective range of product development expenditures per unit sold for a $5 to $10 priced product is $.15 to $.45, for a $10 to $20 priced product it is $.30 to $.90; and for a $20 to $40 product it is $.50 to $1.50. It is important to maintain this budget. A zero budget indicates the product is going to be discontinued, and sales are affected. Product development for one product does carry over for another in the same firm with the result that product development expenditures can be considered to create brand preference for a family of products. (For corporations organized under alternatives B, C, D and E, these product development expenditures do not affect the demand for the products of the corporation's other plants or divisions.)

Competitive Aspects

The relative ranges just described are for the more typical simulations. The activities of the firms strongly influence the total market and the market will develop in accordance with these strategies. For example, if the firms all resort to price-cutting as the primary tactic with little nonprice competition, the market becomes very price sensitive and the low-priced market grows at the expense of the high-priced market. In such a market, a $4 product might be very profitable. Another market might expand by large marketing expenditures and quality improvements. This market would support several high-priced products with large margins and reduce the sales potential of cheap products. This is important to keep in mind for two reasons.

1. Successful tactics in one simulation game are not transferable to subsequent gaming exercises, and you are cautioned to ignore prior good strategies.

2. Market idiosyncrasies can usually be related to the behavior of the other firms in the industry.

Products that are priced very close together will become engaged in a fight for market share, and advertising, sales promotion, product development, and quality will mostly influence selective demand (market share) rather than primary (total industry) demand.

Note, however, that such intense interproduct competitions cannot be provoked merely by the strategem of positioning your product close in price to a group of competitors' products unless a substantial number of your units are actually available for sale.

Market Research

A firm that plans to introduce a new product or modify an established product may purchase research of a test-market nature to obtain information on potential demand. You may test the potential product unit sales for the four demand determinants or any combination thereof. The demand determinants are price, quality (labor and materials value), advertising, and product development expenditures. If you wish to modify an existing product, you may test one or more of these determinants. However, if you plan to use market research prior to introducing a new product, you must test at least two determinants, one of which must be price.

To obtain such information, you must indicate on the decision sheet the prices, total cost per unit, product development, or advertising budget you are considering assigning to your new or changed product. When you are obtaining market information for a proposed product and are willing to buy information for only one, two, or three determinants, the values for the unspecified determinants will be average figures for roughly similar products in your industry. For example, on a new product you might want to know the expected demand for an $18 product at $9 cost per unit with an advertising budget of $120,000 per quarter. You would allocate $75,000 to the new product market research budget and define the $18, $9, and $120,000 in the appropriate blanks. The product development budget for this product will be an average of the product development budgets of the four or five closest priced products at that time. Similarly, when obtaining information for an existing product using fewer than four determinants, the values of the unspecified determinants will be a rough average of those products actually on the market in the period in which you obtain the market research data.

The cost for market research is as follows:

Number of Demand Determinants	Market Research Budget
One	$20,000
Two	45,000
Three	75,000
Four	95,000

This market research information indicates the number of units that a mature product of these characteristics would have sold in the prevailing market conditions of this period.

Available Goods

Production volume from the assembly department during the current period, plus finished goods inventory on hand, determine goods available. Because sales are not at an even rate during the period, you should produce an adequate amount to exceed the total orders received by about 10 percent. If a customer's order is not filled at once he usually will reorder a similar product offered by another firm and not come back.

Goods carried over from one period to another tend to become less saleable, especially in the case of relatively high-quality products. For instance, a one-period old unit produced at $10 roughly matches in saleability a newly manufactured unit costing only $9.40 (i.e., $.60 less). This obsolescence effect is not reflected in the accounting evaluation of inventory.

Chapter 3
Production Environment

The successful formulation of a firm's strategy will depend in part on your understanding of feasible alternatives for your manufacturing capacity. The attainment of your strategy will depend on how carefully you control the resources available. The following sections describe in detail what decisions are required for you to transform raw materials into finished goods available for sale in your market.

You will have to make decisions that include all the economic aspects of a production process. These will include deciding whether to maintain manufacturing capacity or to expand it by purchasing buildings and equipment, when to hire men or fire them, and how to assign men to the two departments of each product. You will have to determine a production rate for both departments. There are costs both in terms of dollars and inefficiencies associated with changes in production rate, expanding manufacturing capacity, and changing the number of men available.

Note carefully that the following activities are not permissible for organizational alternatives B, C, D and E.

1. Buildings and equipment acquired for one plant or division cannot be transferred to another plant or division of the corporation (except indirectly through the vehicle of transfer pricing which is discussed later).

2. Raw materials, purchased parts, fabricated parts and work-in process inventories of one plant or division cannot be transferred to another plant, or division of the corporation.

Buildings and Equipment

Buildings and equipment depreciates at a rate of 2.5 percent per quarter. Depreciation is allocated to the individual products on the basis of direct labor hours and is listed as *depreciation* in the income statements. To maintain a given buildings and equipment value (and thus capacity), you must invest a sum each period equal to the depreciation loss. Buildings and equipment *cannot* be sold. However, you can reduce your buildings and equipment by not replacing the depreciated amounts.

Increasing Buildings and Equipment

You may increase your manufacturing capacity by investing $2,500 (above the amount needed to hold ground against depreciation) in buildings and equipment for each desired additional worker. There is a time lag associated with a decision to increase the size of your manufacturing capacity. The costs of added building and equipment will not be deducted from your plant's cash account until the first period after you have recorded your purchase on the decision sheet. The new capacity will not be available for production until the beginning of the second period after your entry. Depreciation at the expanded rate will commence in the quarter you pay for the addition.

To illustrate, a firm with $1,500,000 in buildings and equipment and a labor force of 600 wishes to increase its labor force to 650 men.

	Investment required
To hold ground against depreciation (0.025 X $1,500,000) =	$ 37,500
For new men (50 X $2,500) =	125,000
Total required purchase of buildings and equipment	$162,500

If this decision is entered on the decision form for period six, the expenditures will be made in period seven, and the new capacity will be available for production during period eight.

Certain assessments are associated with the purchase of buildings and equipment. The following table indicates their approximate magnitude

Investment in buildings and equipment	0	$125,000	$200,000	$1,000,000
Assessment	0	$ 7,000	$ 20,000	$ 250,000

The increasing rate reflects the fact that a sudden expansion of facilities creates expenses such as maintenance, increased need for expediting material, and interruption of normal activities.

The foregoing costs are allocated to individual products proportionately to direct labor hours and are included under *Maintenance* on the plant income statements (see Exhibit 3, p.31). The assessment is paid in the decision period.

Semifixed Costs Included in Factory Overhead

For every product that you produce you will incur certain semifixed costs for supervision and maintenance (see Exhibit 3). The costs of indirect labor are a function of the total labor hours utilized for each product. The cost of supervision depends on the number of workers assigned to a product and is approximately $160 per man. The cost of maintenance depends on the total number of units produced in each product line.

Inventories

A first-in, first-out policy is followed on all inventories during a period. The value of the fabricated parts inventory is based on the raw materials cost per unit plus the fabrication labor cost per unit. Similarly, the value of the assembly department work-in-process inventory and of the finished goods inventory is based on fabricated parts costs, plus purchased parts cost per unit and assembly labor cost per unit. If all inventory from a previous period is not utilized in a given period, its next period value is a weighted average of the old inventory plus inventory purchased or produced during the period.

Labor Force

Your total workforce should have an approximate ratio of one man for each $2500 of buildings and equipment. You may employ an excess of labor, but when the excess reaches approximately 8 percent of the foregoing ratio, added men interfere with the normal production process. This interference results in productivity losses that soon cancel the potential output of the additional labor. All departments lose this productivity in proportion to the number of men assigned.

Employees must be assigned separately to each department of each product. The number of men needed within a department to produce at a given rate is dependent on the labor cost per unit, and the degree of efficiency of the men assigned.

Experienced Men. Men who have been assigned previously to a department of a product produce 500 hours of work per quarter at a rate of $1.80 per hour. For example, if you have scheduled 8000 units of production with a department, and the labor cost per unit is $5.40, you would need forty-eight men (three hours per unit × 8000 units/500 hours per man).

You may schedule in advance any number of overtime hours up to 25 percent of your total number of productive hours in a department for a product. In the foregoing example, if only forty-four men were previously assigned and no additional men were to be hired, 2000 hours of overtime would have to be scheduled in order to meet the production rate. Overtime labor is paid $3 per hour for assembly and $3.60 per hour for fabrication. However, the extra cost of overtime labor is not reflected in the labor value of the product; each overtime labor hour adds only $1.80 labor value to the product. Scheduled overtime is utilized as required to meet scheduled production levels. It will not be utilized until required to achieve the desired output with the assigned number of men. The cost of scheduled overtime is charged whether or not the overtime is actually required to meet the scheduled production rate.

Transferred Men. Men may be shifted from one department and/or product to another. You may make such transfers simply by recording on the decision sheet the total number of men you want to work in each department of each product for the period. [Men may not be shifted between plants under any circumstances for corporation organized under alternatives B, C, D and E.]

Transferred men will not work at full efficiency (i.e., 500 hours of work per quarter) in the first quarter after transfer. Their efficiency depends on the department from which they were transferred. The most efficient transfer is when workers from one department go to the corresponding department in another product. In such a transfer the men would work at about 95 percent efficiency in the period following the transfer. The next most efficient transfer occurs when workers transfer from one department to the other within the same product line. In such a transfer, men would work at about 85 percent efficiency. The least efficient transfer is from one department and product to another department and product. In such a transfer, workers would produce at about 75 percent efficiency. There is no way to indicate on the decision sheet where or how men are to be transferred. The model assumes that workers will be moved in the most efficient manner, and will therefore first transfer men within the same department whenever possible, then within a product line, and so forth. These estimates are provided to enable careful planning of production schedules and do not require any decisions on your part.

Hiring and Firing Men. If you wish to increase your work force, you may hire men at an initial cost of $200 per man. For their first quarter of work, they will work at an average of 55 percent of standard output. You may also release men at a severance cost of $50 per man. As with transferred men, workers are hired or fired to or from a specific department of a specific product. Nonassigned men (idle men) cannot be fired. Hiring or firing requires an additional entry on the decision sheet. Transferring men requires only that the number of men assigned to each department be changed. Hired men should also be included in the total number of men assigned to each department.

Idle Men. If there are more men employed than the total number assigned to the products, the excess men are assigned to a pool of idle men that are paid the usual wage, $1.80 per hour. Men from this pool are available to work in any department on any product at 95 percent efficiency the next quarter. Idle men are assigned to work in a department only after all possible transfers between departments and products are made. The charge for these idle men is apportioned in indirect labor costs of the products in direct proportion to direct labor hours utilized.

Scheduling Production

One of your managerial tasks will be to schedule production of your firm's products. Each decision period represents twelve weeks of productive capacity. The manufacturing process is divided into two stages: fabrication and assembly. The workers assigned to the fabrication department turn raw materials into fabricated parts — fabrication takes three weeks. The assembly department's workforce combines these fabricated parts with purchased parts to produce the finished products — assembly takes two weeks. Figure 1 shows this process together with the six classifications of inventory.

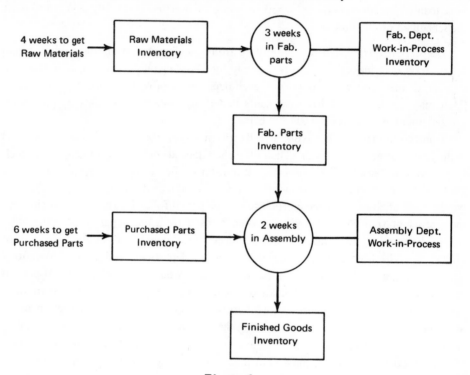

Figure 1

In scheduling the appropriate levels of production, you first must determine what production rates per product are needed to meet anticipated demand for this period and for the next period. Based on these production rates, a sufficient number of raw materials and purchased parts to meet your production schedule for each product will be purchased. Note as shown in the diagram that there are known delays in acquiring raw materials and purchased parts. Therefore, accurate planning of the present and following period's desired output is essential to obtain sufficient inventories to prevent production stoppages due to inventory shortages. To maintain a constant level of production at the beginning of the period, you must have a four-week supply of raw materials and a six-week supply of purchased parts. An automatic purchaser will provide an adequate supply of parts for your defined rates.

In scheduling the rates of production, you should be cognizant of the typical lag times in the total production process. The minimum lot size that can be withdrawn from the fabricated parts inventory is one week's assembly production. This, in effect, sets the minimum level on the size of your fabricated parts inventory by an appropriate amount. If you fail to do so, there will be a temporary work stoppage in the assembly department until the fabricated parts inventory builds up to one week of the higher level of production. Appendix A discusses in detail a procedure that may be used to forecast your production.

Warehousing and Shipping

Packing and shipping costs are about $.10 for each unit sold. Finished goods inventory carrying costs, including warehousing, insurance, and so forth, are approximately $.03 per unit, plus one percent of the inventory valuation per quarter. Raw material and purchased parts inventory carrying costs are about one and one half percent of the inventory valuation per period; fabricated parts and work-in-process inventory carrying costs are about $.03 per unit. These costs are included under *warehousing and shipping* in the income statements.

A new product may be introduced in one of two ways

Introducing a new product

1. If the firm is manufacturing only two products, a third product may be added to the present product line. Each firm may manufacture up to three products simultaneously.

2. One of the current products may be phased out and replaced with a new product. A change of more than 30 percent in the price of a product from one period to the next is considered by the market to be a change of product.

The steps required to implement either of these alternatives follows.

To Add a New Product

1. If market research is used prior to the introduction of the product or during the first period it is on the market, you must test at least two of its four demand determinants (price, quality, advertising, and product development expenditures), one of which must be price.

2. If additional building and equipment capacity must be purchased to support the product's production, it must be ordered at least two periods before it is available for production.

3. Sales promotion expenditures should begin in the period prior to the one in which the product is introduced to the market. Unless substantial changes are made in

the product's price, quality, or product development expenditures in the following period, it will be most effective to discontinue sales promotion expenditures and begin advertising expenditures.

4. Product development expenditures should be started the period before the product is introduced to the market.

5. If you desire to produce but not market a product in a period, this may be done by leaving the price blank.

To Replace a Current Product with a New Product

1. Surplus raw materials, purchased parts, fabricated parts and W.I.P. items may be sold by placing a minus one on the decision sheet under *production rate next period* or when a zero appears under production rate for both this period and the next. They will be sold at the previous average cost minus handling costs.

2. In the period following the one disposal of the old inventories, production rates for the new product may be stated and its production started.

3. Sales promotion expenditures should begin in the period prior to the one that the new product is introduced to the market.

4. Product development expenditures should be continued during the entire transition period.

Chapter 4
Financial Environment

It will be necessary to finance your firm's working capital and long-term capital needs. Several sources of funds are available. Internal sources of funds are provided by depreciation, profits after tax, and working capital changes. External funds can be provided by several forms of debt, as well as by sale of common stock.

In setting your firm's objectives and in developing your competitive strategies to achieve these objectives, you must take into account the impact these goals and the policies will have on your need for funds and the ramification of your fund requirements on the stock price.

The effectiveness of the formulation and execution of your financial policies will be reflected in the market price of your firm's common stock. Seven factors (not necessarily listed in order of importance) are used in determining stock price.

1. The amount of earnings per share;

2. The ability of the firm to deliver steady earnings growth;

3. The firm's over-all rate of return on total assets;

4. The dividend payout ratio;

5. The ability of the firm to produce profits at a previously forecasted level;

6. The ratio of debt to total capitalization;

7. The book value per share.

Each quarter, decisions must be made regarding the acquisition of external funds, where necessary, to finance your working capital and long-term capital needs.

The sources of external funds for the firm are as follows:

1. Ninety-day unsecured loans.

2. Ninety-day secured loans.

3. Ninety-day distress loans.

4. One-year loans.

5. Five-year notes.

6. Common stock.

In general, the ninety-day unsecured loans, one-year loans, and five-year notes will be granted only to those firms that meet fairly demanding tests of financial condition and earnings. If the financial position of a firm that has five-year notes outstanding subsequently deteriorates significantly, the notes outstanding may be retired prematurely in full, at the end of the quarter.

The cash from requested loans is received at the beginning of the quarter. Cash from sales of stock and planned sale of securities is received at the end of the quarter. At either the beginning of the period or at the end, if additional cash is needed, securities will be sold automatically or ninety-day secured or distress loans will be granted. Interest payments are made at the end of each quarter. Interest on loans incurred on the last day of the quarter will be paid in the next quarter.

Loan requests are processed in the following order:

1. Ninety-day unsecured loans.

2. One-year loans.

3. Five-year notes.

4. Other ninety-day loans.

The quick ratios used to test the ninety-day unsecured and one-year loans are calculated as follows:

1. Present cash and notes payable figures are adjusted to reflect the payment of any notes due at the beginning of the period. (Not infrequently this will leave the firm with a negative cash position.)

2. The notes payable figure is adjusted to reflect sinking fund requirements due within the next four quarters.

3. The size of the requested loan plus that of any already granted loans are added to the cash and notes payable accounts.

4. The ratio is then calculated by adding the adjusted cash, securities, and accounts receivable figures and dividing this total by the sum of the accounts payable, taxes payable, and adjusted notes payable figures.

The following paragraphs outline in detail the requirements a firm must meet to use each external source of capital.

1. *Ninety-day Unsecured Loans.* These loans take the form of ninety-day notes with interest at an annual rate of 6 percent and will be available only when requested in advance. To be eligible for such loans a firm must meet the following requirements.

   a. Liquidity. The firm's quick ratio, if the loan is granted, must exceed 1.2.

   b. Profitability. Profits must have been earned in the previous quarter.

   c. Borrowing history. A corporation cannot have ninety-day loans of any form in four consecutive periods.

2. *Ninety-day Secured Loans.* These take the form of ninety-day notes bearing interest at an annual rate of 12 percent. Use of this source may be either planned or unplanned; i.e., emergency financing will be supplied automatically if planned financing is either inadequate or unavailable because the more rigorous financial tests associated with preferred sources of credit cannot be met. These funds will be provided in amounts sufficient to keep the cash balance at a minimum of 5 percent of the quarter's cash expenditures. However, before unplanned loans are made, securities held by the firm, if available, will be sold in amounts sufficient to meet cash requirements. To be eligible for a secured loan, a firm must meet the following requirement.

   a. Collateral. Ninety-day secured loans must not exceed 80 percent of finished goods inventory plus accounts receivable. This ratio is calculated on a pro forma basis by estimating the values of the finished goods inventory plus accounts receivable at the end of the quarter.

3. *Ninety-day Distress Loans.* When such loans are required, they will be made available in the form of ninety-day notes bearing interest at an annual rate of 20 percent. Such funds will be provided automatically and, therefore, need not be ordered. Securities will be sold automatically before distress loans are ordered.

4. *One-Year Loans.* These are one-year notes bearing interest at an annual rate of 7 percent. These notes will be available only if ordered. To be eligible for one-year notes, a corporation must meet the following tests.

   a. Liquidity. The firm's quick ratio if the loan is granted must exceed 1.2.

   b. Profitability. Profits must have been earned in at least three of the four previous quarters.

   If the firm fails any of these tests, no loan will be granted.

5. *Five-Year Notes.* These are five-year notes at an annual interest rate of 7.5 percent. These notes are available only if ordered. These notes require a quarterly sinking fund of one twentieth of the original issue, beginning in the sixth quarter following the issuance of the note with the unpaid balance retired in the twentieth quarter.

   In the second period following the issuance of the note, an amount equal to the quarterly sinking fund is included in current liabilities. To be able to sell notes, a firm must meet the following criteria:

a. Fixed charges coverage. The average cash flow must exceed the fixed charges over the year ending with the current quarter. As computed by the following formula, the fixed charges coverage must be greater than one:

$$\frac{\textit{Profit before taxes} + \textit{Depreciation}}{\dfrac{\textit{sinking fund} + \text{Interest}}{(1 - \text{tax rate})}}$$

Note: The profit before tax figure is an average of the current plus previous three quarter earnings before taxes; the depreciation figure is the current quarter's depreciation; the sinking fund figure is the current quarter's sinking fund plus the quarter sinking fund if the note in question is issued; and the interest figure is the current quarter's interest plus the quarterly interest if the note is issued.

b. Capitalization. Five-year notes may not exceed 30 percent of total assets.

If the firm in unable to meet these tests when its loan application is made, the firm will receive funds from other sources as required. If, during the life of a five-year note, a firm fails to meet 80 percent of either of the foregoing tests (i.e., if the fixed charges coverage ratio is less than 80 percent or five-year notes exceed 44 percent of total assets), any five-year notes outstanding will be repaid immediately. If the firm does not have the cash to cover the accelerated unpaid principal, the firm will automatically have securities sold and if necessary be advanced the required amount in either a ninety-day secured or distress loan.

6. *Common Stock.* Firms may sell stock at any time specifically planned. To sell stock the firm must specify the net dollar amount it wants to raise. On the basis of the seven elements of value discussed earlier, a stock price as of the end of the period will be calculated. This price is then reduced to reflect the dilution of value by the increased number of shares outstanding. The number of new shares needed to obtain the desired funds is calculated to the nearest 100 shares. The cash from the stock sale will be available on the last day of the period. Securities cannot be purchased with funds from the sale of stock in the same period.

7. *Securities.* Firms may invest in interest-bearing securities. These securities earn interest at an annual rate of 6 percent. *Purchase or sale of securities creates side costs of about one half of one percent of the transaction.* Purchases or planned sales of securities are made at the end of the period; interest accumulates during the period securities are held or sold but not for the period in which they are purchased. Securities will automatically be sold if distress loans are required.

Chapter 5

Management Reports

Organizational Structure A

This chapter describes the decision forms and the accoutning reports for Organizational Structure A. (Your instructor will tell you which organizational structure you are operating under.) Under Organizational Structure A, you and two to four of your classmates will manage one of five to seven manufacturing firms that compete directly with each other in the market served solely by you and your competitors. A chart of a five-firm industry is shown in Figure 2 (p. 24).

At the beginning of each quarter you will prepare a decison form similar to that shown in Exhibit 1 (p.25). This form identifies the specific action steps that you are taking to guide your firm during the period. The top line on the decision form is for identification. Complete information as to industry, firm, and period is essential to the administration of the simulation.

Decision form

The succeeding title lines identify the information to be entered in the box directly below the title. Each line will be punched on an IBM card. Card 1 contains financial decisions for the firm. Cards 2–4 are the Product 1 decisions; cards 5–7 for Product 2, and cards 8–10 for Product 3. The following paragraphs discuss the form's layout and the technical procedures to be followed in filling it out.

Financial Decisions (Card 1)

Box 1. The number of $1000 of plant and equipment to be ordered, e.g., $50,000 = 50.

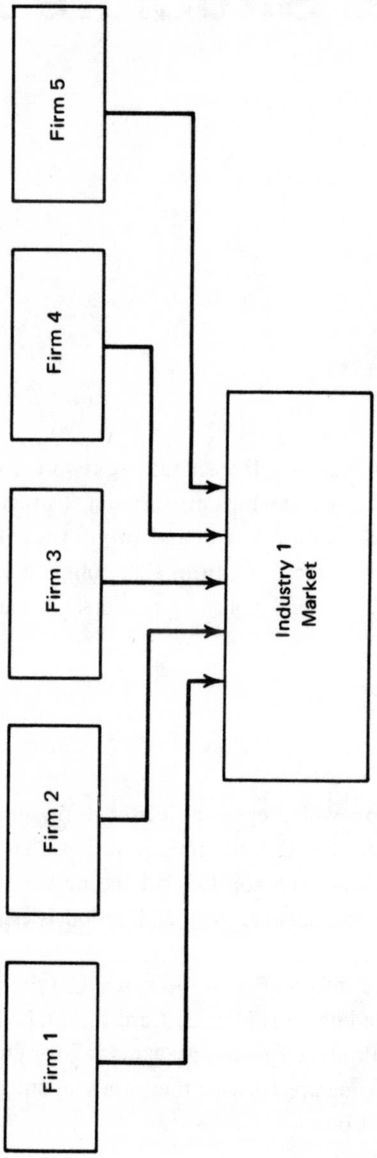

Figure 2

Exhibit 1

MANAGEMENT SIMULATION – DECISION FORM

Industry _____42_____ Firm _____1_____ Period _____1_____

Purchase Plant $1000	Purchase Securities $1000	Dividends $1000	90-Day Loans $1000	One-Year Loan $1000	Five-Year Notes $1000	Sell Stock $1000	
5 0.	0.	1 0 0.	1 0 0.	0.	0.	0.	1

PRODUCT 1

Price Next Period $ per unit	Advertising Budget $1000	Promotion Budget $1000	Prod. Dev. Budget $1000	Mkt. Res. Budget ¢ PU	MR— Price ¢ PU	MR— Adv. $1000	MR— Qual. ¢ PU	MR— P. D. $1000	
7. 7 0	4 3 0.	1 5 0.	5 0.	0.	0.	0.	0.	0.	2

Raw Mat'l $ per unit	Fab. Production Rates Next Pd. 1000 units	This Pd. 1000 units	Fab. Labor $ per unit	Fab. # Men Assigned	# Men Hired Or Fired (−)	Fab. Overtime # Hours	
1. 1 0	2 4 0.	2 4 0.	1. 0 0	2 6 0.	0.	0.	3

Purchased Parts $ per unit	Asm. Production Rates Next Pd. 1000 units	This Pd. 1000 units	Asm. Labor $ per unit	Asm. # Men Assigned	# Men Hired Asm. Or Fired (−)	Asm. Overtime # Hours	
4 0	2 4 0.	2 4 0	.7 0	1 8 2.	0.	1 2 0 0.	4

PRODUCT 2

Price Next Period $ per unit	Advertising Budget $1000	Promotion Budget $1000	Prod. Dev. Budget $1000	Mkt. Res. Budget $1000	MR— Price ¢ PU	MR— Adv. $1000	MR— Qual. ¢ PU	MR— P. D. $1000	
2 0.0 0	8 0.	0.	2 2.	4 5.	1 8 0 0.	0.	9 0 0.	0.	5

Raw Mat'l $ per unit	Fab. Production Rates Next Pd. 1000 units	This Pd. 1000 units	Fab. Labor $ per unit	Fab. # Men Assigned	# Men Hired Fab. Or Fired (−)	Overtime # Hours	
2. 2 0	6 0.	6 0.	2. 4 0	1 3 0.	0.	1 6 6 0 0.	6

Purchased Parts $ per units	Asm. Production Rates Next Pd. 1000 units	This Pd. 1000 units	Asm. Labor $ per unit	Asm. # Men Assigned	# Men Hired Asm. Or Fired (−)	Overtime # Hours	
.6 5	6 0.	6 0.	4. 5 0	2 3 5.	0.	2 6 0 0 0.	7

PRODUCT 3

Price Next Period $ per unit	Advertising Budget $1000	Promotion Budget $1000	Prod. Dev. Budget $1000	Mkt. Res. Budget $1000	MR— Price ¢ PU	MR— Adv. $1000	MR— Qual. ¢ PU	MR— P. D. $1000	
0.	0.	0.	0.	0.	0.	0.	0.	0.	8

Raw Mat'l $ per unit	Fab. Production Rates Next Pd. 1000 units	This Pd. 1000 units	Fab. Labor $ per unit	Fab. # Men Assigned	# Men Hired Fab. Or Fired (−)	Overtime # Hours	
0.	0.	0.	0.	0.	0.	0.	9

Purchased Parts $ per unit	Asm. Production Rates Next Pd. 1000 units	This Pd. 1000 units	Asm. Labor $ per unit	Asm. # Men Assigned	# Men Hired Asm. Or Fired (−)	Overtime # Hours	
0.	0.	0.	0.	0.	0.	0.	10

Box 2.   Securities purchase indicated by a plus (+), sales indicated by a minus (−).

Box 3.   Dividends are paid in multiples of $1000, e.g., $100,000 = 100.

Boxes 4–7. The number of $1000 desired, e.g., $100,000 = 100. Loans are retired automatically and thus retirements should not be indicated here. Similarly you may not buy back your stock.

Marketing Decisions (Cards 2, 5, and 8)

Box 1.   Price of product in dollars per unit for the next period, e.g., $7.70 = 7.70.

Box 2.   The advertising budget in thousands of dollars, e.g., $430,000 = 430.

Box 3.   The promotion budget in thousands of dollars, e.g., $150,000 = 150.

Box 4.   The product development budget in thousands of dollars, e.g., $50,000 = 50.

Box 5.   The market research budget in thousands of dollars, e.g., $65,000 = 65.

Box 6A. Price to be tested by market research in cents per unit, e.g., $18.00 = 1800.

Box 6B. Advertising budget to be tested by market research in $1000, e.g., $100,000 = 100.

Box 7A. Quality of product = sum of fabrication and assembly labor/unit costs plus cost per unit of raw material and purchased parts, to be tested by market research in cents per unit, e.g., $9.00 = 900.

Box 7B. Product development budget to be tested by market research in $1000.

Fabrication Department Decisions (Cards 3, 6, and 9)

Box 1.   Cost per unit of raw material to be purchased, e.g., $1.10 = 1.10.

Box 2.   Scheduled production rate in thousands of units for the following period. This must be filled in to ensure enough raw materials being available for the first four weeks of the next period, e.g., 240,000 units/quarter = 240.

Box 3.   Scheduled production rate in thousands of units at end of period (per Appendix A actual production in period may be considerably less) e.g., 240,000 units/period = 240.

Box 4.   Labor is scheduled on a per unit basis, e.g., $1.00 = 1.00. The quality level will be met and the quantity of units produced will be reduced if there are not enough productive hours available.

Box 5.   The *total* number of men assigned to a department of a product. This *includes* men previously assigned *plus or minus* men hired or fired *plus* men transferred from another department and/or product.

Box 6.   Number of new employees desired to be hired specifically for that product (+) or number of employees working for that product to be released (−) from the firm.

Box 7.   Total number of overtime hours desired, e.g., 12,000 = 12000.

Assembly Department Decisions (Cards 4, 7, and 10)

Format identical to cards 3, 6, and 9 with purchased parts in place of raw materials.

Exhibit 2 (p.28) contains a copy of a product statement. Three of those are prepared each quarter, one for each product line. The following paragraphs identify the significance of key items on the report in order of their appearance.

Product statement

REVENUE FROM SALES = price times sales volume for the product concerned.

COST OF GOODS SOLD AT STANDARD COSTS—The sum of the following five items.

FABRICATION LABOR	Standard unit cost of items sold if there have been no
ASSEMBLY LABOR	= changes. Weighted average standard unit cost of items sold
RAW MATERIALS	during periods when changes are being effected.
PURCHASED PARTS	

OVERTIME PREMIUM = *Additional* cost of overtime hours scheduled at $1.80 per hour for fabrication department and $1.20 per hour for assembly department.

GROSS PROFIT = revenue from sales—cost of goods sold at standard cost

FACTORY OVERHEAD

INDIRECT LABOR = $900 × number of idle men + labor inefficiency costs.

SUPERVISION = About $160 per worker.

MAINTENANCE = Depends on total assembly department production volume, about $200 per 1000 units produced for low volumes, $300 per 1000 units for high-volume production + sales costs of increasing plant capacity.

DEPRECIATION = 2.5 percent of plant value allocated on the basis of direct labor hours.

Exhibit 2

I N D U S T R Y 41   F I R M   2   P R O D U C T   1

I N C O M E   S T A T E M E N T   P E R I O D   2

REVENUE FROM SALES, AT $ 5.65 PER UNIT		$ 1957838.
THE PRICE DECISION FOR NEXT PERIOD IS 5.65		
COST OF GOODS SOLD AT STANDARD COST		
FABRICATION LABOR, AT $ 0.99 PER UNIT	342643.	
ASSEMBLY LABOR, AT $ 0.62 PER UNIT	216139.	
RAW MATERIALS, AT $ 1.10 PER UNIT	381172.	
PURCHASED PARTS, AT $ 0.40 PER UNIT	139605.	
OVERTIME PREMIUM	0.	1079559.
GROSS PROFIT		878279.
FACTORY OVERHEAD		
INDIRECT LABOR	0.	
SUPERVISION	12565.	
MAINTENANCE	21229.	
DEPRECIATION	8053.	41847.
MARKETING AND ADMINISTRATIVE EXPENSES		
ADVERTISING	100000.	
SALES PROMOTION	0.	
COMMISSIONS AND SALESMENS EXPENSE	133892.	
WAREHOUSE AND SHIPPING	56959.	
PRODUCT DEVELOPMENT	50000.	
MARKET RESEARCH	0.	
ADMINISTRATIVE	41468.	382319.
OPERATING PROFIT		$ 454112.

P R O D U C T I O N

	FABRICATION DEPT.	ASSEMBLY DEPT.
PRODUCTION VOLUME, UNITS	90000.	100800.
W.I.P. INVENTORY, UNITS	22500.	16800.
NUMBER OF MEN HIRED OR FIRED	0.	0.
NUMBER OF MEN BUDGETED	41.	28.
NUMBER OF MEN WORKING	41.	28.
NUMBER OF HOURS AVAILABLE	20500.	14000.
PERCENT HOURS UTILIZED	100.	100.
NUMBER OF HOURS OVERTIME	0.	0.

I N V E N T O R I E S

RAW MATERIALS AT $ 0.74 PER UNIT, 33333. UNITS		
PURCHASED PARTS AT $ 0.37 PER UNIT, 50000. UNITS		
FABRICATED PARTS AT $ 1.15 AVERAGE PER UNIT 77236. UNITS		
FINISHED GOODS, IN UNITS		
BEGINNING		745207.
PRODUCTION		108600.
GOODS AVAILABLE		853807.
ORDERS RECEIVED	346520.	
SALES LOST	0.	
SALES VOLUME		346520.
ENDING, AT $ 2.89 AVERAGE COST PER UNIT		507287.
SHARE OF INDUSTRY UNIT SALES VOLUME, PERCENT		23.

MARKETING AND ADMINISTRATIVE EXPENSE

ADVERTISING, SALES PROMOTION, PRODUCT DEVELOPMENT, AND MARKET RESEARCH	= Budgets (i.e., entries on decision form prepared for period.
COMMISSIONS AND SALESMEN'S EXPENSES	= Commission rate of 5 percent of dollar sales + about $.15 per unit sold.
WAREHOUSE AND SHIPPING	= $.03 per unit of total work in process and fabricated parts inventories on hand plus $.03 per unit of finished goods inventory plus one percent of the finished goods inventory evaluation plus $.10 per unit sold plus one and a half percent of the value of raw material and purchased parts inventories on hand.
ADMINISTRATIVE	= One administrator for about every 50,000 units produced in each department (i.e., Product 1, Assembly, Product 1, Fabrication, and so forth) at about $16,000 per year. Plus one top executive for each million dollars worth of plant at an average salary of about $25,000 per year allocated to products on the basis of direct labor hours plus costs associated with hiring and firing men and handling securities. In cases of decreasing production, administrators are laid off at the rate of about 20 percent of the extra men being dismissed each period.

OPERATING PROFIT = GROSS PROFIT — FACTORY OVERHEAD — SELLING AND ADMINISTRATIVE EXPENSES

PRODUCTION

This report covers both fabrication and assembly departments separately.

PRODUCTION VOLUME, UNITS	= Number of units that enter that department during period.
W.I.P. INVENTORY, UNITS	= Number of units in process at end of period, i.e., fabrication department, three weeks' amount of production, assembly department, two weeks' amount.
NUMBER OF MEN BUDGETED	= Actual entries made on decision form for period.
NUMBER OF MEN WORKING	= Actual number of men working in department in period. This number will be smaller than the number of men budgeted only when you try to assign more workers than you have available in your work force.
NUMBER OF HOURS AVAILABLE	= Five hundred hours per man previously assigned and less for men transferred or hired plus NUMBER OF HOURS OVERTIME (see labor force, production.)

PERCENT HOURS UTILIZED $=$ An indicator of the efficiency of the labor force

$$= \frac{\text{number of standard hours needed for period's production}}{\text{NUMBER OF HOURS AVAILABLE}}$$

INVENTORIES

FINISHED GOODS, PRODUCTION $=$ Number of units completed by assembly department

SHARE OF INDUSTRY SALES VOLUME, PERCENT $=$ Percent of total industry unit sales generated by this product.

MARKET RESEARCH

SALES $=$ Number of units.

Income Statement, Plant Report, and Business Index

Exhibit 3 contains a copy of the company's income statement, which is prepared each quarter. At the bottom of this statement, data are presented on the firm's plant status and the business index. Down through operating profit, this income statement simply totals the values on the individual product reports (see Exhibit 2). The other entries are determined as follows:

INTEREST EXPENSE $=$ financial interest

SECURITY INCOME $=$ Earned and entered at the rate of 1 percent per period, on the value of securities held throughout each period.

TAXABLE INCOME $=$ OPERATING PROFIT $+$ SECURITY INCOME $-$ INTEREST EXPENSE

INCOME TAX $=$ 52 percent of taxable income. There is an immediate tax rebate in case of loss up to the amount of taxes your firm has paid.

NET INCOME $=$ TAXABLE INCOME $-$ INCOME TAX

The plant report summarizes the value of buildings and equipment during the period following the date of the report. You will want to use this in determining the maximum total labor force for next period, i.e., one man per $2500 buildings and equipment. The **TOTAL NUMBER OF EMPLOYEES** for this period is also shown. This is the total of men assigned to each department plus idle men, if any. The total number of men in the **IDLE LABOR POOL** is identified separately.

GAIN FROM NEW INVESTMENT $=$ Buildings and equipment purchase decision last period.

Exhibit 3

M A N A G E M E N T   S I M U L A T I O N

I N D U S T R Y   41   F I R M   2

I N C O M E   S T A T E M E N T   P E R I O D   2

TOTAL SALES REVENUE $ 2488510.

COST OF GOODS SOLD
    FABRICATION LABOR   408977.
    ASSEMBLY LABOR   315640.
    RAW MATERIALS   437556.
    PURCHASED PARTS   156188.
    OVERTIME PREMIUM   0.   1318361.

G R O S S   P R O F I T   1170149.

FACTORY OVERHEAD
    INDIRECT LABOR   40822.
    SUPERVISION   80416.
    MAINTENANCE   35544.
    DEPRECIATION   50311.   207092.

MARKETING AND ADMINISTRATIVE EXPENSES
    ADVERTISING   150000.
    SALES PROMOTION   5000.
    COMMISSIONS AND SALESMENS EXPENSE   164926.
    WAREHOUSE AND SHIPPING   69416.
    MARKET RESEARCH   0.
    PRODUCT DEVELOPMENT   85000.
    ADMINISTRATIVE   79095.   553436.

OPERATING PROFIT   409620.

INTEREST EXPENSE   26082.
SECURITY INCOME   0.
TAXABLE INCOME   383538.
INCOME TAX   199440.

N E T   I N C O M E $ 184098.

P L A N T   R E P O R T

PLANT CAPACITY, PERIOD   3 $ 2013120.
LOSS FROM DEPRECIATION   50328.
GAIN FROM NEW INVESTMENT   51000.
PLANT CAPACITY, PERIOD   4 $ 2013792.

TOTAL NUMBER OF EMPLOYEES   470.
IDLE LABOR POOL   0.

B U S I N E S S   I N D E X   (SEASONALLY ADJUSTED)

PERIODS −1 TO 2 (ACTUAL)	616	612	640	654
PERIODS 3 TO 6 (ESTIMATED)	646	618	591	591
PERIODS 7 TO 10 (ESTIMATED)	584	610	639	645

Balance Sheet, Financial Ratios, and Cash Flow Worksheet

Exhibit 4 contains a copy of the company's balance sheet which is prepared each quarter. Underneath the balance sheet are a set of financial ratios and a cash flow worksheet. The following paragraphs identify how each of the items on the report is calculated.

BALANCE SHEET

CASH
= Former value of same item plus net cash inflow for the period (which of course represents a reduction when negative).

SECURITIES
= Former value of same item plus purchase (or minus for sale) of securities during the period concerned.

ACCOUNTS RECEIVABLE
= Approximately 30 percent of sales of current period.

INVENTORIES
= The sum of the inventory valuation for individual products.

CURRENT ASSETS
= The sum of the four items just listed.

PLANT AND EQUIPMENT, NET = The end-of-period value of plant minus depreciation. This is the value the maximum number of efficient employees is dependent upon for the next period.

TOTAL ASSETS
= current assets + plant and equipment, net

ACCOUNTS PAYABLE
= About thirty day's worth of raw material and purchased parts purchases and one third of the advertising budget.

NOTES PAYABLE
= Total of all loans and notes due within one year, including portion of five-year notes due within one year.

TAXES
= Amount of taxes owned. In case of a loss, there is an immediate rebate, if tax credits exist.

CURRENT LIABILITIES
= The sum of the three items just listed.

LONG-TERM DEBT
= Amount of five-year notes not due within one year.

COMMON STOCK
= Number of shares and total par value.

SURPLUS
= Retained earnings.

TOTAL LIABILITIES AND EQUITY = CURRENT LIABILITIES plus three items just listed.

Financial Ratios

1. TOTAL LIABILITIES TO TOTAL ASSETS $= \dfrac{\text{CURRENT LIABILITIES} + \text{LONG-TERM DEBT}}{\text{TOTAL ASSETS}}$

2. LONG-TERM DEBT TO TOTAL ASSETS = SELF-EXPLANATORY.

3. QUICK RATIO $= \dfrac{\text{CASH} + \text{SECURITIES} + \text{ACCOUNTS RECEIVABLE}}{\text{CURRENT LIABILITIES}}$

4. CURRENT RATIO $= \dfrac{\text{CURRENT ASSETS}}{\text{CURRENT LIABILITIES}}$

Exhibit 4

```
        I N D U S T R Y  41     F I R M   2

        B A L A N C E   S H E E T     P E R I O D   2
CASH                                              71497.
SECURITIES                                            0.
ACCOUNTS RECEIVABLE                              873161.
INVENTORIES
    RAW MATERIALS             105025.
    PURCHASED PARTS            50092.
    WORK IN PROCESS           208646.
    FABRICATED PARTS          189154.
    FINISHED GOODS           1642504.           2195421.
CURRENT ASSETS                                  3140079.
PLANT AND EQUIPMENT, NET                         2013120.

T O T A L   A S S E T S                         5153199.

ACCOUNTS PAYABLE                                 149921.
NOTES PAYABLE                                     895479.
TAXES                                            199440.
CURRENT LIABILITIES                             1244840.
LONG TERM DEBT                                        0.
COMMON STOCK             500000. SHARES         1600000.
SURPLUS                                          2308358.

T O T A L   L I A B I L I T I E S   A N D   E Q U I T Y    5153199.
```

TOTAL LIAB TO TOTAL ASSETS	LONG TERM DEBT TO TOTAL ASSETS	QUICK RATIO	CURRENT RATIO	FIXED CHARGES COVERAGE
24 0/0	0 0/0	0.76	2.52	2.50

STOCK PRICE $ 7 1/8

```
        C A S H   F L O W   W O R K S H E E T

CASH FLOW OPERATIONS                             459931.
TAX EXPOSURE                                     239164.
TAX SHIELD (DEPRECIATION)                         26162.
CAPITAL EXPENDITURES PLANT                        51000.

CASH PROFILE                                     195928.

CHANGES IN NON CASH WORKING CAPITAL             -563898.
INTEREST (NET OF TAX SHIELD)                      12519.
DIVIDENDS PAID                                        0.
REPAYMENT OF 90 DAY LOANS                       1654792.
REPAYMENT OF ONE YEAR LOAN                            0.
REPAYMENT OF FIVE YEAR NOTE                           0.
CASH FROM 90 DAY SECURED LOAN, ISSUED BEGINNING OF PERIOD    793097.
CASH FROM 90 DAY SECURED LOAN, ISSUED END OF PERIOD          102382.

NET CHANGE IN CASH BALANCE                       -12005.
```

5. FIXED CHARGES COVERAGE = $\dfrac{\text{Average* profit before taxes} + \text{depreciation} + \dfrac{\text{sinking fund}}{(1 - \text{tax rate})} + \text{Interest}}{}$

6. STOCK PRICE = Dollars per share.

CASH FLOW STATEMENT

CASH FLOW OPERATIONS

Sum of the operating profit plus depreciation plus security income.

TAX EXPOSURE

CASH FLOW OPERATIONS multiplied by tax rate (0.52)

TAX SHIELD (DEPRECIATION)

DEPRECIATION multiplied by 0.52

CAPITAL EXPENDITURES (PLANT)

Cash payments in period for plant and equipment

CASH PROFILE

CASH FLOW OPERATIONS − TAX EXPOSURE + TAX SHIELD DEPRECIATION − CAPITAL EXPENDITURES

CHANGES IN NONCASH AND DEBT WORKING CAPITAL

Net change between this period and last period in ACCOUNTS RECEIVABLE, INVENTORIES, ACCOUNTS PAYABLE, and TAXES PAYABLE

Other entries are obvious.

Industry Report

Exhibit 5 contains a copy of the company's industry report. Each firm in an industry receives the identical industry report, which presents gross statistics on all competitors in the industry. The data presented under the titles PROFIT AND LOSS and FINANCIAL CONDITION are expressed in $1000 and are accurate. The data under individual products with the exception of PRICE and PRICE NEXT PER are *not* accurate but have been randomized. This gives you an indication of what other firms are doing, but prevents the immediate identifying of shifts in tactics. In most instances these figures are within 20 percent of their actual value.

PRICE and DIRECT CPU are in dollars: ADVERTISING (which includes promotion) and PRODUCT develop budgets are $1000 and SALES UNITS are in 1000s. Products 1, 2, and 3 are listed from left to right.

*This period and three periods.

Exhibit 5

I N D U S T R Y 41   P E R I O D   2

I N D U S T R Y   R E P O R T

F I R M   1
STOCK PRICE $ 6 7/8
DIVIDENDS PAID   0.

PROFIT AND LOSS		FINANCIAL COND		INDIVIDUAL PRODUCTS		
SALES RVNUE	2501.	CASH	106.	PRICE	17.00	7.00	0.00
TOT EXPENSE	2209.	INVENTORY	2476.	ADVERTISNG	85.00	301.75	0.00
OPER PROFIT	292.	PLANT-EQUP	2029.	PROD DEVEL	34.00	51.00	0.00
SECURTY INC	0.	TOT LIAB	2150.	DIRECT CPU	6.80	2.68	0.00
NET EARNED	118.	COM EQUITY	3338.	SLS UNITS	39.18	208.52	0.00
				PRICE NEXT PER	17.00	7.00	0.00

F I R M   2
STOCK PRICE $ .7 1/8
DIVIDENDS PAID   0.

PROFIT AND LOSS		FINANCIAL COND		INDIVIDUAL PRODUCTS		
SALES RVNUE	2489.	CASH	71.	PRICE	5.65	16.00	0.00
TOT EXPENSE	2079.	INVENTORY	2195.	ADVERTISNG	85.00	42.50	4.25
OPER PROFIT	410.	PLANT-EQUP	2013.	PROD DEVEL	42.50	21.25	0.00
SECURTY INC	0.	TOT LIAB	1245.	DIRECT CPU	2.46	6.12	0.00
NET EARNED	184.	COM EQUITY	3908.	SLS UNITS	294.54	28.19	-0.00
				PRICE NEXT PER	5.65	16.00	30.00

F I R M   3
STOCK PRICE $ 5 5/8
DIVIDENDS PAID   100000.

PROFIT AND LOSS		FINANCIAL COND		INDIVIDUAL PRODUCTS		
SALES RVNUE	2206.	CASH	106.	PRICE	8.75	11.00	0.00
TOT EXPENSE	2255.	INVENTORY	2564.	ADVERTISNG	170.00	170.00	42.50
OPER PROFIT	-50.	PLANT-EQUP	2561.	PROD DEVEL	34.00	29.75	0.00
SECURTY INC	0.	TOT LIAB	3416.	DIRECT CPU	2.80	4.68	0.00
NET EARNED	-79.	COM EQUITY	2590.	SLS UNITS	84.84	102.95	0.00
				PRICE NEXT PER	7.50	12.50	30.00

F I R M   4
STOCK PRICE $ 6
DIVIDENDS PAID   0.

PROFIT AND LOSS		FINANCIAL COND		INDIVIDUAL PRODUCTS		
SALES RVNUE	2407.	CASH	78.	PRICE	8.50	14.00	0.00
TOT EXPENSE	2150.	INVENTORY	1404.	ADVERTISNG	229.50	102.00	0.00
OPER PROFIT	256.	PLANT-EQUP	2010.	PROD DEVEL	23.80	29.75	0.00
SECURTY INC	0.	TOT LIAB	1038.	DIRECT CPU	3.27	6.25	0.00
NET EARNED	113.	COM EQUITY	3299.	SLS UNITS	144.91	58.13	0.00
				PRICE NEXT PER	8.50	14.00	0.00

F I R M   5
STOCK PRICE $ 6 7/8
DIVIDENDS PAID   50000.

PROFIT AND LOSS		FINANCIAL COND		INDIVIDUAL PRODUCTS		
SALES RVNUE	3250.	CASH	122.	PRICE	6.70	13.20	0.00
TOT EXPENSE	2819.	INVENTORY	2157.	ADVERTISNG	340.00	144.50	0.00
OPER PROFIT	431.	PLANT-EQUP	2006.	PROD DEVEL	55.25	42.50	0.00
SECURTY INC	0.	TOT LIAB	1966.	DIRECT CPU	2.74	5.02	0.00
NET EARNED	187.	COM EQUITY	3459.	SLS UNITS	273.15	70.65	0.00
				PRICE NEXT PER	6.70	13.20	0.00

Chapter 6
Management Reports and Internal Financial Decisions
Organizational Structures B and C

This chapter describes the organizational and reporting structure for firms operating under Organizational Structures B and C. (Your instructor will advise you as to which organizational structure you are operating under.) The chapter covers three topics:

1. The exact details of Organizational Structure B and C.

2. The procedures for transferring cash within a company.

3. The decision forms and accounting reports prepared and used by firms with Organizational Structures B and C.

Organizational structure B

You and a group of your classmates will manage a corporation that has two divisions. Your corporation will compete directly against other corporations, each of which also has two divisions. The two divisions of your corporation will each compete in a different market (a market may best be visualized as being a distinct geographic area that effectively has no trade interaction with other geographic areas). Thus, the two divisions of your corporation will compete only with divisions of other corporations. A chart of a four-corporation competitive situation is shown in Figure 3. Within the corporation you will become a member of one of two groups.

1. A four- or five-man division.

2. The corporate staff.

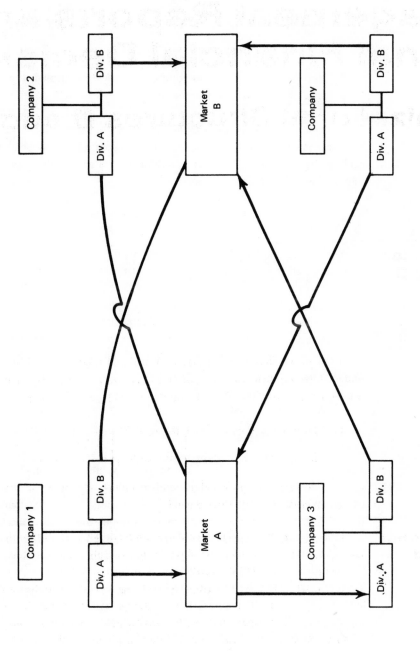

Figure 3

The basic operating entity is the four- or five-man division. Each division will be responsible for planning, producing, and distributing two or three products. These products will compete with those of divisions of other corporations in the market.

The corporate staff will be responsible for:

1. Allocating the corporation's financial resources among the two divisions.

2. Approving divisional budgets.

3. Raising capital for the corporation as necessary through the sale of stock or issuance of bonds and short-term notes.

In reading the rest of the chapter, those sections discussing financial decisions of the firm describe those decisions made at the corporate level. Special attention should be paid to the portion of the finance section that discusses the problem and methods of transferring cash between divisions.

Organization structure C

You and a group of your classmates will manage a corporation that has three divisions. Your corporation will compete directly against other corporations, each of which also has three divisions. The three divisions of your corporation will each compete in a different market (a market may best be visualized as being a distinct geographic area that effectively has no trade interaction with other geographic areas). Thus, the three divisions of your corporation will compete only with divisions of other corporations. See Figure 4 (p.39) for a chart of competitive relations. Within the corporation you will become a member of one of two groups:

1. A four- or five-man division.

2. The corporate staff.

The basic operating entity is the four- or five-man division. Each division will be responsible for planning, producing, and distributing two or three products. These products will compete with those divisions of other corporations in the market. In reading the rest of the manual, those sections that talk about the firm's marketing and production activities describe the division level activities and decisions. The corporate staff will be responsible for:

1. Allocating the corporations' financial resources among the two divisions.

2. Approving capital for the corporation as necessary through the sale of stock or issuance of bonds and short-term notes.

In reading the rest of the manual, these sections discussing financial decisions of the firm describe those decisions made at the corporate level. Special attention should be paid to the portion of the finance section that discusses the problem and methods of transferring cash between divisions.

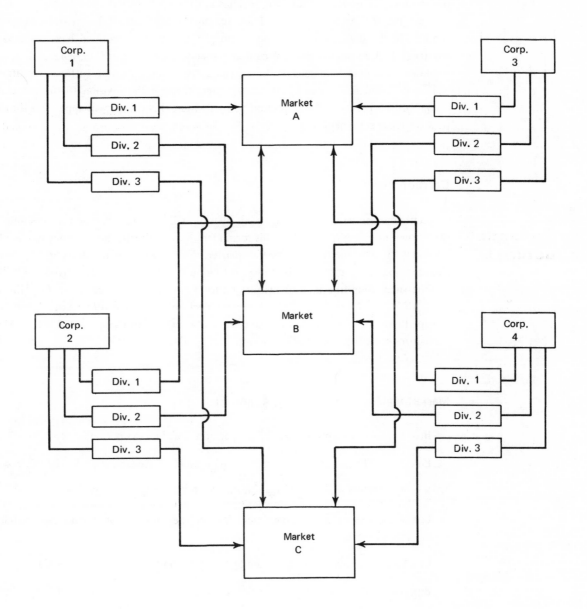

Figure 4

Cash transfers

Each quarter the corporation must decide how much, if any, cash should be granted to or taken from each division.

Cash may be transferred between headquarters and the divisions *without a charge* only at the start of a quarter. The only restriction in the amount transferred is that a minimum balance of $50,000 be kept at corporation headquarters. (Note there is no minimum cash requirement for divisional headquarters.)

Cash raised through ninety-day loans acquired at the start of the quarter may be distributed to the division and/or used to fulfill the minimum required balance at headquarters. If a division is short of cash at the end of the quarter (i.e., if its ending cash position is less than 5 percent of the quarter's cash disbursements), sufficient additional will be provided automatically by headquarters through the division to the plant at a charge of one percent of the amount so provided. This charge will appear on the corporate income statement.

Decision Forms

At the beginning of the quarter each division will prepare a decision form similar to that shown in Exhibit 6 (p.41). This form identifies the specific action steps that are being taken to guide the firm during the quarter. The top line of the decision form is for identification and complete information as to industry, corporation, and division.

The succeeding title lines identify the information to be entered in the box directly below the title. Lines 1–3 are for Product 1 decisions; lines 4–6 for Product 2; and lines 7–9 for Product 3. The following paragraphs discuss the form's layout and the technical procedures to be followed in filling it out.

Marketing Decisions (Lines 1, 4, and 7)

Box 1. Price of product in dollars per unit, for the next period, e.g., $7.70 = 7.70.

Box 2. The advertising budget in thousands of dollars, e.g., $430,000 = 430.

Box 3. The promotion budget in thousands of dollars, e.g., $50,000 = 50.

Box 4. The product development budget in thousands of dollars, e.g., $50,000 = 50.

Box 5. The market research budget in thousands of dollars, e.g., $45,000 = 45.

Box 6A. Price to be tested by market research in cents per unit, e.g., $18.00 = 1800.

Box 6B. Advertising budget to be tested by market research, in $1000.

Box 7A. Quality of product = sum of fabrication and assembly labor budgets plus cost per unit of raw material and purchased parts, to be tested by market research, in cents per unit, e.g., $9.00 = 900.

Box 7B. Product development budget to be tested by market research.

Exhibit 6

MANAGEMENT SIMULATION — DIVISION DECISION FORM

Industry ___1___ Corporation ___1___ Division ___1___ Period ___4___

PRODUCT 1

Price Next Period $ per unit	Advertising Budget $1000	Promotion Budget $1000	Prod. Dev. Budget $1000	Mkt. Res. Budget $1000	MR— Price ¢ PU	MR— Adv. $1000	MR— Qual. ¢ PU	MR— P. D. $1000	
7.70	430.	0.	50.	0.	0.	0.	0.	0.	2

Raw Mat'l $ per unit	Fab. Production Rates Next Pd. 1000 units	This Pd. 1000 units	Fab. Labor $ per unit	Fab. # Men Assigned	# Men Hired Or Fired (−)	Fab. Overtime # Hours	
1.10	200.	200.	1.00	260.	0.	0.	3

Purchased Parts $ per unit	Asm. Production Rates Next Pd. 1000 units	This Pd. 1000 units	Asm. Labor $ per unit	Asm. # Men Assigned	# Men Hired Or Fired (−)	Asm. Overtime # Hours	
40	200.	200.	.70	182.	0.	0.	4

PRODUCT 2

Price Next Period $ per unit	Advertising Budget $1000	Promotion Budget $1000	Prod. Dev. Budget $1000	Mkt. Res. Budget $1000	MR— Price ¢ PU	MR— Adv. $1000	MR— Qual. ¢ PU	MR— P. D. $1000	
20.00	80.	0.	22.	45.	1800.	0.	900.	0.	5

Raw Mat'l $ per unit	Fab. Production Rates Next Pd. 1000 units	This Pd. 1000 units	Fab. Labor $ per unit	Fab. # Men Assigned	# Men Hired Or Fired (−)	Fab. Overtime # Hours	
2.20	60.	60.	2.40	130.	0.	16600.	6

Purchased Parts $ per units	Asm. Production Rates Next Pd. 1000 units	This Pd. 1000 units	Asm. Labor $ per unit	Asm. # Men Assigned	# Men Hired Or Fired (−)	Asm. Overtime # Hours	
65	60.	60.	450.	235.	0.	26000.	7

PRODUCT 3

Price Next Period $ per unit	Advertising Budget $1000	Promotion Budget $1000	Prod. Dev. Budget $1000	Mkt. Res. Budget $1000	MR— Price ¢ PU	MR— Adv. $1000	MR— Qual. ¢ PU	MR— P. D. $1000	
0.	0.	0.	0.	0.	0.	0.	0.	0.	8

Raw Mat'l $ per unit	Fab. Production Rates Next Pd. 1000 units	This Pd. 1000 units	Fab. Labor $ per unit	Fab. # Men Assigned	# Men Hired Or Fired (−)	Fab. Overtime # Hours	
0.	0.	0.	0.	0.	0.	0.	9

Purchased Parts $ per unit	Asm. Production Rates Next Pd. 1000 units	This Pd. 1000 units	Asm. Labor $ per unit	Asm. # Men Assigned	# Men Hired Or Fired (−)	Asm. Overtime # Hours	
0.	0.	0.	0.	0.	0.	0.	10

41

Fabrication Department Decisions (Lines 2, 5, and 8)

Box 1. Cost per unit of raw material to be purchased, e.g., $1.10 = 1.10.

Box 2. Scheduled production rate in 000s of units for the following period. This must be filled in to ensure enough raw materials being available for the first four weeks of the next period, e.g., 240,000 units = 240.

Box 3. Scheduled rate of production in 000s of units for period (per Appendix A actual production may be considerably less) e.g., 265,000 units/period = 265.

Box 4. Labor is scheduled on a per unit basis, e.g., $1.00 = 1.00. The quality level will be met, and quantity of units produced will be reduced if there are not enough productive hours available.

Box 5. The *total* number of men assigned to a department of a product. This *includes* men previously assigned *plus or minus* men hired or fired *plus* men transferred from another department and/or product.

Box 6. Number of new employees desired (+) or number of employees to be released (−) from the firm.

Box 7. Total overtime hours desired, e.g., 12,000 = 12000.

Assembly Department Decisions (Lines 3, 6, and 9)

The format is identical to lines 2, 5, and 8 with purchased parts in place of raw materials.

Corporate Decision Form

Exhibit 7 (p.44) is a copy of the decision form that must be filled out each quarter for the company as a whole. This form identifies the external financial, building and equipment, and cash transfer decisions for the company. It also requires a forecast of earnings per share.

The top line of the decision form is for identification, and complete information here as to corporation number and period is essential to the administration of the simulation.

The succeeding title lines identify the information to be entered in the box directly below the title. Each line will be punched on an IBM card.

External Financial Decisions (Line 1)

Box 1. Securities purchase decision indicated by a plus (+), sale indicated by a minus (−).

Box 3-6. The number of $1000 desired, e.g., $200,000 = 200. Loans are retired automatically.

Forecasted Earnings/Share (Line 2)

Boxes 1-4. Respectively will contain your forecasted earnings per share for each of the next four periods.

Buildings and Equipment Purchases (Line 3)

Boxes 1-3. Respectively will contain the number of $1000 of buildings and equipment purchased for each of the corporation's divisions.

Cash Transfers to and from Division (Line 4)

Boxes 1-3. Will indicate the amount of cash to be transferred between each division and headquarters. Cash to be transferred *to* the division *from* headquarters will be signified by a plus (+) sign. Cash to be transferred *from* the division *to* headquarters will be signified by a minus (−) sign.

Product Statement

Exhibit 8 (p.46) contains a copy of a product statement. Three of these are prepared for each division every quarter, one for each product line. The following paragraphs identify the significance of key items on the report in the order of their appearance.

REVENUE FROM OUTSIDE SALES = Price times external sales value for the product concerned.

COST OF GOODS SOLD AT STANDARD COST = The sum of the following five items.

FABRICATION LABOR	Standard unit cost of items sold if there have been no
ASSEMBLY LABOR	= changes. Weighted average standard unit cost of items sold
RAW MATERIALS	during periods when changes are being effected.
PURCHASED PARTS	

OVERTIME PREMIUM = Additional cost of overtime hours schedules at $1.80 per hour for fabrication department and $1.20 per hour for assembly department.

GROSS PROFIT = REVENUE FROM SALES − COST OF GOODS SOLD AT STANDARD COST

FACTORY OVERHEAD

INDIRECT LABOR = $900 X number of idle men + labor efficiency variance

SUPERVISION = About $160 per worker.

MAINTENANCE = Depends on total production volume, about $200 per 1000 units produced for low volumes, $200 per 1000 units for high-volume production + side costs of increasing buildings and equipment capacity.

Exhibit 7

MANAGEMENT SIMULATION — CORPORATE DECISION FORM

Corporation _____ **Period** _____

External Financial Decisions					
Purchase Securities ($1000)	Dividends ($1000)	90-Day Loans ($1000)	One Year Loans ($1000)	Five Year Notes ($1000)	Sell Stock ($1000)
/////	/////	/////	/////	/////	/////

Forecasted Earnings Per Share				
This Period	Next Period	Two Periods in Future	Three Periods in Future	/////
/////	/////	/////	/////	/////

Building and Equipment Purchases					
Division 1 ($1,000)		Division 2 ($1,000)		Division 3 ($1,000)	
/////	/////	/////	/////	/////	/////

Cash Transfers to and from Divisions			
Division 1	Division 2	Division 3	/////
			/////

DEPRECIATION = 2.5 percent of buildings and equipment value allocated on the basis of direct labor hours.

MARKETING AND ADMINISTRATIVE EXPENSE

ADVERTISING, PROMOTION, PRODUCT DEVELOPMENT AND MARKET RESEARCH = Budgets (i.e., entries on decision form prepared for period).

COMMISSIONS AND SALESMEN'S EXPENSES = Commission rate of 5 percent of sales dollars + about $.15 per unit sold.

WAREHOUSE AND SHIPPING = Three cents per unit of total work in process and fabricated parts inventories on hand + $.03 per unit of finished goods inventory + one percent of the finished goods inventory evaluation + $.10 per unit sold + one and a half percent of the value of raw material and purchase parts inventories on hand.

ADMINISTRATIVE = One administrator for about every 50,000 units produced in each department (i.e., Product 1, assembly, Product 1, fabrication, and so forth) at about $4000 per period + one top executive for each million dollars worth of buildings and equipment at an average salary of about $25,000 per allocated to products on the basis of direct labor hours + costs associated with hiring and firing men.

OPERATING PROFIT = GROSS PROFIT — FACTORY OVERHEAD — MARKETING AND ADMINISTRATIVE EXPENSES

PRODUCTION

This report covers both fabrication and assembly departments separately.

PRODUCTION VOLUME, UNITS = Number of units that enter that department during period.

W.I.P. INVENTORY, UNITS = Number of units in process at end of period, i.e., fabrication department, three weeks' amount of production, assembly department, two weeks' amount.

NUMBER OF MEN BUDGETED = Actual entries made on decision form for period.

NUMBER OF MEN WORKING = Actual number of men working in department in period. This number will be smaller than the number of men budgeted only when you try to assign more workers than you have available in your work force.

NUMBER OF HOURS AVAILABLE = Five hundred hours per man previously assigned and less for men transferred or hired plus NUMBER OF HOURS OVERTIME.

Exhibit 8

```
        I N D U S T R Y   1           P E R I O D   12
  D I V   2 -                      - C O R P O R A T I O N   3
        P R O D U C T   1   I N C O M E   S T A T E M E N T
```

REVENUE FROM OUTSIDE SALES, AT $ 6.50 PER UNIT $ 1528384.

PRICE NEXT PERIOD $ 6.50 PER UNIT
COST OF GOODS SOLD AT STANDARD COST
    FABRICATION LABOR, AT $ 1.02 PER UNIT   239839.
    ASSEMBLY LABOR,   AT $ 0.62 PER UNIT   145784.
    RAW MATERIALS,   AT $ 1.05 PER UNIT   246893.
    PURCHASED PARTS, AT $ 0.40 PER UNIT   94054.

    OVERTIME PREMIUM   0.   726570.
GROSS PROFIT   801814.

FACTORY OVERHEAD
    INDIRECT LABOR   6.
    SUPERVISION   75390.
    MAINTENANCE   56468.
    DEPRECIATION   43718.   175581.

MARKETING AND ADMINISTRATIVE EXPENSES
    ADVERTISING   345000.
    PROMOTION   0.
    COMMISSIONS AND SALESMENS EXPENSE   115419.
    WAREHOUSE AND SHIPPING   41366.
    PRODUCT DEVELOPMENT   50000.
    MARKET RESEARCH   0.
    ADMINISTRATIVE   55865.   607649.
OPERATING PROFIT $ 18584.

P R O D U C T I O N

	FABRICATION DEPT.	ASSEMBLY DEPT.
PRODUCTION VOLUME, UNITS	245292.	249672.
W.I.P. INVENTORY, UNITS	61323.	41612.
NUMBER OF MEN HIRED OR FIRED	-52.	-24.
NUMBER OF MEN BUDGETED	278.	172.
NUMBER OF MEN WORKING	278.	172.
NUMBER OF HOURS AVAILABLE	139000.	86000.
PERCENT HOURS UTILIZED	100.	100.
NUMBER OF HOURS OVERTIME	0.	0.

I N V E N T O R I E S

RAW MATERIALS AT $ 1.05 PER UNIT, 82002. UNITS
PURCHASED PARTS AT $ 0.40 PER UNIT, 126828. UNITS
FABRICATED PARTS AT $ 2.07 AVERAGE PER UNIT 39635. UNITS
FINISHED GOODS, IN UNITS
    BEGINNING   114965.
    PRODUCTION   255480.

    GOODS AVAILABLE   370445.
    ORDERS RECEIVED   235136.
    SALES LOST   0.
    INTERNAL SALES VOLUME
    SALES VOLUME   235136.
    ENDING, AT $ 3.09 AVERAGE COST PER UNIT   135309.
SHARE OF INDUSTRY UNIT SALES VOLUME, PERCENT   8.

PERCENTAGE HOURS UTILIZED = An indicator of the efficiency of labor force

$$= \frac{\text{number of hours needed for period's production}}{\text{NUMBER OF HOURS AVAILABLE}}$$

INVENTORIES

FINISHED GOODS, PRODUCTION = Number of units completed by assembly department.

SHARE OF INDUSTRY SALES VOLUME, PERCENT = Percent of total industry unit sales generated by this product

MARKET RESEARCH

SALES = Number of units.

Division Income Statement

Exhibit 9 (p.49) is a copy of the income statement prepared for each division every period. This report summarizes income figures, plant status, and the business index.

INCOME STATEMENT

This simply totals the individual product reports.

PLANT REPORT

Directly below the income statement in Exhibit 9 is a plant report summarizing the value of buildings and equipment during the period following the date of the report. You will want to use this in determining the maximum total labor force for the next period, i.e., one man per $2500 in buildings and equipment. The TOTAL NUMBER OF EMPLOYEES for this period is also shown. This should be the total of men assigned to each department plus idle men, if any. The total number of men in the IDLE LABOR POOL is identified separately.

GAIN FROM NEW INVESTMENT = Buildings and equipment purchase decisions last period.

BUSINESS INDEX

The values of the index are precise for present and past periods, but the accuracy of the forecasted values decrease as they become longer range.

Division Balance Sheet and Cash Flow Statement

Exhibit 10 (p.50) contains copies of the divisional balance sheets and cash flow statements which are prepared each period. The following paragraphs identify how each of the items on the report is calculated.

BALANCE SHEET

CASH = Former value of the same item plus net cash inflow for the period (which, of course, represents a reduction when negative).

ACCOUNTS RECEIVABLE = Approximately 30 percent of the sales of the current period.

INVENTORIES = The sum of the inventory valuation for individual products.

CURRENT ASSETS = The sum of the four items just listed.

BUILDINGS AND EQUIPMENT, NET = The end-of-period value of buildings and equipment minus depreciation. This is the value the maximum number of efficient employees is dependent upon for the next period.

TOTAL ASSETS = CURRENT ASSETS + BUILDINGS AND EQUIPMENT, NET.

ACCOUNTS PAYABLE = About thirty days' worth of raw material and purchased parts purchases and one third of the marketing budget.

CASH FLOW

Those items which may be difficult to understand are explained below.

CASH SALES = Cash sales made during period to outside customers.

CASH FROM ACCOUNTS RECEIVABLE = Opening accounts receivable, usually about 30 per cent of sales of prior period.

CASH FROM CORPORATION = Cash supplied by corporation to sustain division's operations. It is automatically provided in amounts necessary to pay all due bills and sustain the division's minimum cash balance.

TOTAL CASH EXPENDITURES = MARKETING AND ADMINISTRATIVE EXPENSES + SUPERVISION AND MAINTENANCE COSTS + $900 X total number of men + total cost of overtime + opening accounts payable − closing accounts payable + raw material and purchased parts purchases.

Industry Report

Exhibit 11 (p. 54) contains a copy of the division's industry report. Each division in an industry receives the identical industry report which presents gross statistics on all competitors in an industry. The data presented under the titles profit and loss and financial condition are expressed in $1000 and are accurate. The data under individual product with the exception of PRICE and PRICE NEXT PER are not accurate but have been randomized. This gives you an indication of what other divisions are doing but prevents the immediate identifying of shifts in tactics. In most instances these figures are within 20 percent of their actual values.

PRICE and DIRECT CPU are in dollars ADVERTISING (which includes promotion) and PRODUCT DEVELOP budgets are $1000 and SALES UNITS are in 1000s. Products 1, 2, and 3 are listed from left to right.

Exhibit 9

M A N A G E M E N T   S I M U L A T I O N

I N D U S T R Y   1 - C O R P O R A T I O N   3 - D I V I S I O N   2

I N C O M E   S T A T E M E N T   P E R I O D   12

TOTAL SALES REVENUE $ 4289611.

COST OF GOODS SOLD
   FABRICATION LABOR   588338.
   ASSEMBLY LABOR   476751.
   RAW MATERIALS   592899.
   PURCHASED PARTS   221380.

   OVERTIME PREMIUM   0.   2262468.

G R O S S   P R O F I T   2027143.

FACTORY OVERHEAD
   INDIRECT LABOR   307.
   SUPERVISION   138215.
   MAINTENANCE   79847.
   DEPRECIATION   77891.   296260.

MARKETING AND ADMINISTRATIVE EXPENSES
   ADVERTISING   750000.
   PROMOTION   84000.
   COMMISSIONS AND SALESMENS EXPENSE   289481.
   WAREHOUSE AND SHIPPING   73904.
   MARKET RESEARCH   0.
   PRODUCT DEVELOPMENT   108000.
   ADMINISTRATIVE   104968.   1410353.

N E T   I N C O M E $ 320531.

   B U I L D I N G S   A N D   E Q U I P M E N T   R E P O R T
BUILD/EQUIP CAPACITY, PERIOD   13 $ 3037754.
LOSS FROM DEPRECIATION   75944.
GAIN FROM NEW INVESTMENT   0.
BUILD/EQUIP CAPACITY, PERIOD   14 $ 2961810.
TOTAL NUMBER OF EMPLOYEES   802.

   B U S I N E S S   I N D E X   (SEASONALLY ADJUSTED)

PERIODS 9 TO 12 (ACTUAL)		675	678	685	692
PERIODS 13 TO 16 (ESTIMATED)		711	721	733	748
PERIODS 17 TO 20 (ESTIMATED)		731	771	759	760

Exhibit 10

B A L A N C E   S H E E T   P E R I O D   12

I N D U S T R Y   1 - C O R P O R A T I O N   3 - D I V I S I O N   2

CASH		143824.
ACCOUNTS RECEIVABLE		1415713.
INVENTORIES		
RAW MATERIALS	135904.	
PURCHASED PARTS	79621.	
WORK IN PROCESS	419385.	
FABRICATED PARTS	188699.	
FINISHED GOODS	836172.	
		1659781.
CURRENT ASSETS		3219318.
BUILDINGS AND EQUIPMENT, NET		3037754.
T O T A L A S S E T S		6257072.
ACCOUNTS PAYABLE		423636.
DIFFERENCE BETWEEN TOTAL ASSETS AND TOTAL LIABILITIES		5833435.

C A S H   F L O W

CASH SALES	2873898.
CASH FROM ACCOUNTS RECEIVABLE	1382915.
CASH FROM	0.
T O T A L R E C E I P T S	4256813.
TOTAL CASH EXPENDITURES	2876480.
CAPITAL EXPENDITURES, BUILDINGS AND EQUIPMENT	
CASH TO	1010277.
T O T A L D I S B U R S E M E N T S	4269857.
N E T C A S H I N F L O W	-13044.

Corporation Income Statement

Exhibit 12 (p. 55) contains a copy of the company's income statement, which is prepared each period. At the bottom of the income statement is a summary of the corporation's plant status and the same business index figures as on the division income statements.

Down through OPERATING PROFIT, this simply totals the individual division income statements (see Exhibit 9, p. 49). The other entries are determined as follows:

INTEREST EXPENSE = financial interest

BANK CHARGES—emergency cash = one percent of the amount of emergency loans made to divisions at the end of the period to maintain minimum cash balances.

SECURITY INCOME = Earned and entered at the rate of one percent per period, on the value of securities held throughout each period.

TAXABLE INCOME = OPERATING PROFIT + SECURITY INCOME − INTEREST EXPENSE

INCOME TAX = 52 percent of taxable income. There is an immediate tax rebate in case of loss up to the amount of taxes your firm has paid.

NET INCOME = taxable income − income tax

The plant report is simply a combination of the information on the divisional plant report.

CORPORATION BALANCE SHEET AND CASH FLOW STATEMENT

Exhibit 13 (p. 56) contains a copy of the company's balance sheet which is prepared each quarter. Underneath the balance sheet are a set of financial ratios and a cash flow statement. The following paragraphs identify how each of the items on the report is calculated.

BALANCE SHEET

CASH − HEADQUARTERS

CASH DIVISION = Former value of same item plus net cash inflow for the period (which of course represents a reduction when negative). (Sum of cash balances appearing on divisional balance sheets).

SECURITIES = Former value of the same item plus purchase (or minus sale) of securities during the period concerned.

ACCOUNTS RECEIVABLE = Approximately 30 percent of the sales of current period. (Sum of ACCOUNTS RECEIVABLES on divisional balance sheets.)

INVENTORIES = The sum of the inventory valuation for individual products (appearing on divisional balance sheets).

CURRENT ASSETS = The sum of the four items just listed.

BUILDINGS AND EQUIPMENT, NET = The end-of-period value of plant minus depreciation (sum of buildings and equipment on divisional balance sheets). This is the value the maximum number of efficient employees is dependent upon for the next period.

51

TOTAL ASSETS = CURRENT ASSETS + BUILDINGS AND EQUIPMENT, NET

ACCOUNTS PAYABLE = About thirty days' worth of raw material and purchased parts purchases and one third of the advertising budget. (Sum of accounts payable on divisional balance sheets.)

NOTES PAYABLE = Total of all loans and notes due within one year, including portion of five-year notes due within one year.

TAXES = Amount of taxes owed. In case of a loss, there is an immediate rebate, if tax credits exist, which will show under the cash flow receipts. In case of a profit, the tax owed will appear her to be paid next period.

CURRENT LIABILITIES = The sum of the three items just listed.

LONG-TERM DEBT = Amount of five-year notes not due within one year.

COMMON STOCK = Number of shares and total par value.

SURPLUS = retained earnings.

TOTAL LIABILITIES AND EQUITY = current liabilities plus the three items just listed.

FINANCIAL RATIOS

1. TOTAL LIABILITIES TO TOTAL ASSETS = $\dfrac{\text{CURRENT LIABILITIES} + \text{LONG-TERM DEBT}}{\text{TOTAL ASSETS}}$

2. LONG-TERM DEBT TO TOTAL ASSETS = SELF-EXPLANATORY.

3. QUICK RATIO = $\dfrac{\text{cash} + \text{securities} + \text{accounts receivable}}{\text{current liabilities}}$

4. CURRENT RATIO = $\dfrac{\text{current assets}}{\text{current liabilities}}$

5. FIXED CHARGES COVERAGE = $\dfrac{\text{average* profit before taxes} + \text{depreciation}}{\dfrac{\text{sinking fund}}{(1 - \text{tax rate})} + \text{Interest}}$

STOCK PRICE = Dollars per share.

CASH FLOW

Most entries are self-explanatory. Note the following, however.

CASH FROM ACCOUNTS RECEIVABLE = Opening accounts receivable, normally about 30 percent of the sales of prior period.

INCOME FROM SECURITIES = One percent of the value of securities held or sold this period.

CASH FROM SECURITIES, NOTES, AND STOCK = Appear only when applicable.

*This period and last three periods

TOTAL CASH EXPENDITURES = MARKETING AND ADMINISTRATIVE EXPENSES + INTEREST + SUPERVISION AND MAINTENANCE COSTS + $900 × total number of men + TOTAL COST OF OVERTIME + opening accounts payable — closing accounts payable + raw material and purchased parts purchases.

REPAYMENT OF FIVE-YEAR NOTE = Amount of five-year note repaid during this period.

Divisional Report

Exhibit 14 (p. 57) contains a summary of the information on the divisional reports (i.e., income statement, balance sheets, and product line statements) for use by the corporate staff. This report is prepared each period.

Most items, with the exception of those in the cash flow statement, are self-explanatory.

OPERATIONS = Cash sales + collection of accounts receivable — cash expenses.

CORPORATION = Cash given to or taken from the division at the beginning of the period by headquarters.

DSTRSS CASH = Cash given to the division at the end of the period by headquarters because cash level is below required minimum.

PLANT PUR = Cash outlays of plant purchase during period.

CASH DECREASE, CASH INCREASE = Net change in the division's cash balance over the course of the period.

PRODUCT LINE REPORT

This report presents summary data on the performance of each of the division's product lines. The entries under mfg stat may be interpreted as follows:

PROD VOL = Total unit output (in 000s) from the product's assembly department during period.

FGD INV = Number of units (in 000s) in finished goods inventory at the end of the period.

NR MEN = Total number of men working in the product's fabrication and assembly departments during period.

HRS OVTM = Total number of hours ov overtime (in 000s) in the product's fabrication and assembly departments during period.

% UTIL = Average efficiency of workers in the product's fabrication and assembly departments during period.

Exhibit 11

CORPORATION INCOME STATEMENT, DIVISION REPORT
INDUSTRY 41 PERIOD — 2
INDUSTRY REPORT

CORPORATION 1 DIVISION 1

PROFIT AND LOSS		FINANCIAL COND		INDIVIDUAL PRODUCTS		
SALES RVNUE	3552.	CASH	148.	PRICE	8.80	5.75	0.00
TOT EXPENSE	2884.	INVENTORY	1491.	ADVERTISNG	272.00	255.00	0.00
OPER PROFIT	668.	PLANT—EQUP	2580.	PROD DEVEL	38.25	42.50	0.00
		TOT LIAB	2138.	DIRECT CPU	2.72	2.00	0.00
				SLS UNITS	164.27	273.71	0.00
				PRICE NEXT PER	8.80	5.75	0.00

CORPORATION 2 DIVISION 1

PROFIT AND LOSS		FINANCIAL COND		INDIVIDUAL PRODUCTS		
SALES RVNUE	2664.	CASH	114.	PRICE	8.20	13.25	0.00
TOT EXPENSE	2218.	INVENTORY	991.	ADVERTISNG	255.00	85.00	0.00
OPER PROFIT	446.	PLANT—EQUP	2596.	PROD DEVEL	34.00	17.00	0.00
		TOT LIAB	1818.	DIRECT CPU	2.80	5.96	0.00
				SLS UNITS	192.68	51.65	0.00
				PRICE NEXT PER	7.70	13.25	0.00

CORPORATION 3 DIVISION 1

PROFIT AND LOSS		FINANCIAL COND		INDIVIDUAL PRODUCTS		
SALES RVNU	3015.	CASH	121.	PRICE	6.85	16.00	0.00
TOT EXPENSE	2519.	INVENTORY	874.	ADVERTISNG	272.00	93.50	0.00
OPER PROFIT	496.	PLANT—EQUP	2600.	PROD DEVEL	42.50	23.80	0.00
		TOT LIAB	1720.	DIRECT CPU	2.59	6.80	0.00
				SLS UNITS	296.73	33.15	0.00
				PRICE NEXT PER	6.85	16.00	0.00

CORPORATION 4 DIVISION 1

PROFIT AND LOSS		FINANCIAL COND		INDIVIDUAL PRODUCTS		
SALES RVNUE	2941.	CASH	133.	PRICE	5.10	11.25	0.00
TOT EXPENSE	2613.	INVENTORY	1349.	ADVERTISNG	255.00	127.50	0.00
OPER PROFIT	328.	PLANT—EQUP	2593.	PROD DEVEL	51.00	11.90	0.00
		TOT LIAB	2044.	DIRECT CPU	1.87	5.11	0.00
				SLS UNITS	302.73	85.00	0.00
				PRICE NEXT PER	5.10	11.25	0.00

CORPORATION 5 DIVISION 1

PROFIT AND LOSS		FINANCIAL COND		INDIVIDUAL PRODUCTS		
SALES RVNUE	2445.	CASH	298.	PRICE	14.00	5.90	0.00
TOT EXPENSE	2219.	INVENTORY	1220.	ADVERTISNG	97.75	306.00	0.00
OPER PROFIT	226.	PLANT—EQUP	2589.	PROD DEVEL	13.60	27.20	0.00
		TOT LIAB	965.	DIRECT CPU	6.16	2.04	0.00
				SLS UNITS	52.71	227.24	0.00
				PRICE NEXT PER	14.00	5.90	0.00

Exhibit 12

**MANAGEMENT SIMULATION
CORPORATION 1
INCOME STATEMENT PERIOD −3**

TOTAL SALES REVENUE		$ 9843889.
COST OF GOODS SOLD		
FABRICATION LABOR	1467160.	
ASSEMBLY LABOR	1187738.	
RAW MATERIALS	1600447.	
PURCHASED PARTS	584496.	
OVERTIME PREMIUM	0.	
		4839841.
GROSS PROFIT		5004048.
FACTORY OVERHEAD		
INDIRECT LABOR	604742.	
SUPERVISION	939862	
MAINTENANCE	556766.	
DEPRECIATION	356312.	2457682.
MARKETING AND ADMINISTRATIVE EXPENSES		
ADVERTISING	2760000.	
PROMOTION	80000.	
COMMISSIONS AND SALESMENS EXPENSE	765193	
WAREHOUSE AND SHIPPING	372896.	
MARKET RESEARCH	0.	
PRODUCT DEVELOPMENT	409000.	
ADMINISTRATIVE	482592.	4869681.
OPERATING PROFIT		−2323316.
INTEREST EXPENSE		111306.
BANK CHARGES—EMERGENCY CASH		44690.
SECURITY INCOME		0.
TAXABLE INCOME		−2479312.
INCOME TAX		−1289241.
NET INCOME		$ −1190071.

PLANT REPORT

PLANT CAPACITY, PERIOD −2	$ 14252487.
LOSS FROM DEPRECIATION	356312.
GAIN FROM NEW INVESTMENT	365050.
PLANT CAPACITY, PERIOD −1	$ 14261225.
TOTAL NUMBER OF EMPLOYEES	5634.

BUSINESS INDEX (SEASONALLY ADJUSTED)

PERIODS −6 TO −3 (ACTUAL)	700	700	700	664
PERIODS −2 TO 1 (ESTIMATED)	658	650	651	637
PERIODS 2 TO 5 (ESTIMATED)	690	690	673	693

Exhibit 13

CORPORATION 1

BALANCE SHEET PERIOD —3

CASH (HEADQUARTERS)		50000.
CASH (DIVISIONAL)		719348.
SECURITIES		0.
ACCOUNTS RECEIVABLE		3348262.
INVENTORIES		
RAW MATERIALS	1333304.	
PURCHASED PARTS	782253.	
WORK IN PROCESS	2656621.	
FABRICATED PARTS	961694.	
FINISHED GOODS	3876729.	9610601.
CURRENT ASSETS		13728210.
BLDG. AND EQUIPMENT, NET		14252487.
TOTAL ASSETS		17980698.
ACCOUNTS PAYABLE		2203875.
NOTES PAYABLE		4505671.
TAXES		0.
CURRENT LIABILITIES		6709546.
LONG TERM DEBT		0.
COMMON STOCK	3000000. SHARES	14252500.
SURPLUS		7018652.
TOTAL LIABILITIES AND EQUITY		27980698.

TOTAL LIAB TO TOTAL ASSETS	LONG TERM DEBT TO TOTAL ASSETS	QUICK RATIO	CURRENT RATIO	FIXED CHARGES COVERAGE
23 0/0	0 0/0	0.61	2.05	9.92

STOCK PRICE $ 7 1/2

CASH FLOW

CASH SALES	6495627.
CASH FROM ACCOUNTS RECEIVABLE	3832541.
INCOME FROM SECURITIES	0.
TAX REFUND	994345.
CASH FROM 90 DAY SECURED LOAN, ISSUED BEGINNING OF PERIOD	4452244.
CASH FROM 90 DAY SECURED LOAN, ISSUED END OF PERIOD	53427.
TOTAL RECEIPTS	15828184.
TOTAL CASH EXPENDITURES (INCL INTEREST)	14542955.
SECURITIES PURCHASED	0.
CAPITAL EXPENDITURES, PLANT	356300.
DIVIDENDS PAID	875000.
REPAYMENT OF 90 DAY LOANS	0.
REPAYMENT OF ONE YEAR LOAN	0.
REPAYMENT OF FIVE YEAR NOTE	0.
TOTAL DISBURSEMENTS	15774255.
NET CASH INFLOW	53929.

Exhibit 14

CORPORATION 1 — PERIOD—3 — DIVISIONAL REPORT

DIVISION 1 (LOCATED IN INDUSTRY 1)

BALANCE SHEET				CASH FLOW STATEMENT			
ASSETS		LIAB/N.W.		SOURCES		APPLICATIONS	
CASH	240.	ACCT PAY	687.	OPERATIONS	0.	OPERATIONS	1342.
ACCTS REC	998.			DSTRSS CASH	1470	B—EQP PUR	110.
INVENTORY	3511.			CORPORATION	—0.	CORPORATION	0.
BLDG—EQUP—N	2200.			CSH DECREASE	0.	CSH INCREASE	18.
BLDG—EQUP—S	2200.	ASSET—LIAB	8462.	TOTAL	1470.	TOTAL	1470.
TOTAL	9148.	TOTAL	9148.				

INCOME STATEMENT

SALES		2933.
LESS C.G.S.		1246.
GROSS PROFIT		1687.
EXPENSES		
FAC OHD	679.	
M AND A	1771.	2451.
OPER PROF		—764.

PRODUCT LINE REPORT

	1	2	3
EXTERNAL SALES			
PRICE	8.80	5.75	0.
C.P.U.	3.20	2.34	0.
SLS UNITS	100.	177.	0.
ADVERTISING	320.	300.	0.
PROD DEV	45.	50.	0.
OPER PROF	—85.	—157.	0.
MFG STAT			
PROD VOL	219.	376.	0.
FGD INV	144.	240.	0.
NR MEN	408.	472.	0.
HRS OVTM	0.	0.	0.
O/O UTIL	100.	100.	0.

Chapter 7

Management Reports and Internal Financial Decisions

Organizational Structures D and E

This chapter describes the organizational and reporting structure for firms operating under Organizational Structure D or E. (Your instructor will advise you as to which organizational structure you are operating under.) The chapter covers four topics:

1. The exact details of Organization Structures D and E.

2. The procedures for transferring cash within a company.

3. The procedures for transferring products within a company.

4. The decision forms and accounting reports prepared and used by firms with Organization Structures D or E.

Under this organizational structure, you and your classmates will manage a corporation that has two divisions, each of which has two plants. Your corporation will compete against other corporations, each of which also has two divisions with two plants. The two divisions of your corporation will each compete in a different market (a market may best be visualized as being a distinct geographic area that effectively has no trade interactions with other geographic areas). Thus the division of one corporation will compete only with divisions of other corporations as shown in Figure 5 (p. 60). The two plants of a division, however, will both be in the same industry and thus will be directly competitive.

Organization structure D

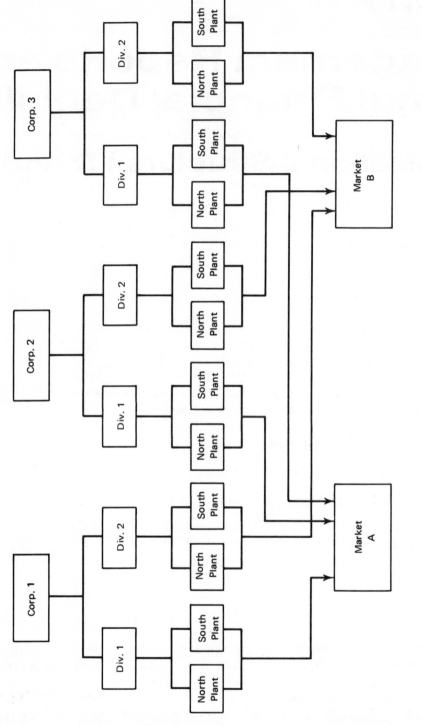

Figure 5

Within the corporation you will become a member of one of the following three groups:

1. A four- or five-man plant.

2. A divisional staff.

3. The corporate staff.

The basic operating entity is the four- or five-man plant. Each plant will be responsible for planning, producing, and distributing two or three products. These products will compete with products produced by five other competing plants in the industry (including the other plant in its division). The divisional staff will be responsible for:

1. Allocating divisional financial resources between other plants.

2. Coordinating plant activities as needed.

3. Approving plant budgets.

The exact nature of the role to be played by this staff is, of course, completely at the discretion of the corporation.

These activities will not result directly in the filling out of any decision form, and members of the staff should be generally familiar with the specific decisions to be made at the corporate and plant levels. The corporate staff will be responsible for:

1. Allocating the corporation's financial resources among its several divisions.

2. Approving divisional budgets.

3. Raising capital for the corporation as necessary through the sale of stock or issuance of bonds and short-term notes.

In reading the rest of the chapter those sections discussing financial decisions of the firm describe those decisions made at the corporate level. Special attention should be paid to the portion of the finance section discussing the problems and methods of transferring cash between divisions and plants.

Organization structure E

You and your classmates will manage a corporation that has three divisions, each of which has two plants. Your corporation will compete directly against other corporations each of which also has three divisions with two plants. The three divisions of your corporation will each compete in a different market (a market best visualized as being a distinct geographic area that effectively has no trade interactions with other geographic areas.

Thus the divisions of one corporation will compete only with divisions of other corporations. The two plants of a division, however, will both be in the same industry and thus will be directly competitive as seen in Figure 6.

Within the corporation you will become a member of one of the following groups:

1. A four- or five-man plant.

2. A division staff.

3. The corporate staff.

The basic operating entity is the four- or five-man plant. Each plant will be responsible for planning, producing, and distributing two or three products. These products will compete with products produced by five other competing plants in the industry (including the other plant in its division). The divisional staff will be responsible for:

1. Allocating divisional financial resources between other plants.

2. Coordinating plant activities as needed.

3. Approving plant budgets.

The exact nature of the role to be played by this staff is, of course, completely at the discretion of the corporation.

These activities will not result directly in the filling out of any decision form, and members of the staff should be generally familiar both with the specific decisions to be made at the corporate and plant levels. The corporate staff will be responsible for:

1. Allocating the corporation's financial resources among its several divisions.

2. Approving divisional budgets.

3. Raising capital for the corporation as necessary through the sale of stock or issuance of bonds and short-term notes.

In reading the rest of the chapter the sections discussing financial decisions of the firm describe those decisions made at the corporate level. Special attention should be paid to the portion of the finance section discussing the problems and methods of transferring cash between divisions and plants.

Cash transfers

Each period the corporation must decide how much, if any, cash should be granted to or taken from each division. (Cash will be transferred automatically between the division cash account and the plants in amounts sufficient to maintain the required minimum cash balance for the plant. Each plant must have a minimum cash balance of at least 5 percent of the current period's cash disbursements.)

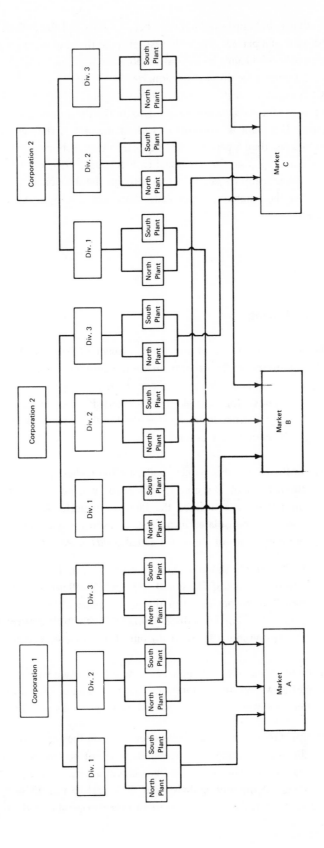

Figure 6

Cash may be transferred between headquarters and the divisions *without a charge* only at the start of a period. The only restriction in the amount transferred is that a minimum balance of $50,000 must be kept at corporation headquarters. (Note there is no minimum cash requirement for division headquarters.)

Cash raised through ninety-day loans acquired at the start of the period may be distributed to the division and/or used to fulfill the minimum required balance at headquarters. If a plant is so short of cash at the end of the period (i.e., if its ending cash position is less than 5 percent of the quarter's cash disbursements) that the difference cannot be made up from the divisional cash account, sufficient additional cash will be provided automatically by headquarters through the division to the plant at a charge of one percent of the amount so provided. This charge will appear on the corporate income statement.

Transfer Pricing

Goods manufactured in one plant, instead of being sold to its external customers, may be sold to one of the other plants of the corporation for sale to its customers. Goods so requested will be available for sale in the requesting plant one quarter after the request is made. Suppose, for example, the Northern Plant of Division 2 requests 10,000 units for its Product 3 from Product 1 of the Southern Plant of Division 1. This request is placed on the Period 10 decision form.

1. In Period 10, this request will take the highest priority in Product 1 of the Southern Plant of Division 1. No goods will be shipped to any outside customers until they have fulfilled the internal request. At the end of the period, these goods will be isolated into a special inventory account on the balance sheet of the Southern Plant of Division 1 called *goods in transit.*

2. In Period 11, the transfer will take place and will be recorded as a sale for the Southern Plant of Division 1. The goods will arrive in the Northern Plant of Division 2 at the beginning of the period and will be available for immediate sale in Period 11. An immediate payment for the entire purchase will be made to the selling division. There is no out-of-pocket cost associated with these transfers.

The unit price at which the transfer will take place will be determined by the appropriate parties within the corporation. The recording of the transfers on the various financial statements will be handled according to generally accepted accounting principles.

1. An interdivisional sale will be reflected on the appropriate product line, plant and divisional income statements. It will not be reflected on the corporate income statement. The transferred goods will appear on the plant and divisional balance sheets of the buying division at their cost to this division. On the corporate balance sheet, they will be restated to their original manufacturing cost.

2. An intradivisional sale will be reflected on the appropriate product line and plant income statements. It will not be reflected in either the divisional or corporate income statements. The transferred goods will appear on the buying plant's balance sheet at their cost to the plant. On the divisional and corporation balance sheets they will be restated to their original manufacturing cost.

Transferred items saleability depend on their original manufacturing costs. For example, if a $7 product has been selling items with $3 of quality in them and it buys from another plant items that cost $2.50 to make, the market will see the product line as downgrading rather than improving its quality, regardless of the internal transfer price.

No more than five transfers are allowed in a period. Transferred goods will be sold immediately upon arrival in the buying division. No items manufactured in the buying product line will be sold until all the transferred items have been sold. If transfers from two or more locations are being brought into a product line, the following rules relate to its disposal.

1. Merchandise transferred from the other plant in the division is sold first.

2. Merchandise transferred from outside the division is sold second. (If two or more outside transfers come in, they are combined in assortments and are sold at an average value.)

3. Merchandise manufactured in the division is sold last.

Advertising, promotion and product development will all help in moving transferred merchandise.

Decision Forms

At the beginning of every period each plant will prepare a decision form similar to that shown in Exhibit 15(p. 66).This form identifies the specific steps that are being taken to guide the firm during the period. The top line of the decision form is for identification, and complete information as to industry, corporation, division, and plant is essential to the administration of the simulation.

The succeeding title lines identify the information to be entered in the box directly below the title. Each line will be punched on an IBM card. Lines 1-3 are for Product 1 decisions; lines 4-6, for Product 2; and lines 7-9, for Product 3. The following paragraphs discuss the form's layout and the technical procedures to be followed in filling it out.

Exhibit 15

MANAGEMENT SIMULATION — PLANT DECISION FORM

Industry ___1___ Corporation ___1___ Div.–Plt. ___1-N___ Period ___4___

PRODUCT 1

Price Next Period $ per unit	Advertising Budget $1000	Promotion Budget $1000	Prod. Dev. Budget $1000	Mkt. Res. Budget $1000	MR– Price ¢ PU	MR– Adv. $1000	MR– Qual. ¢ PU	MR– P. D. $1000	
7. 7 0	4 3 0.	0.	5 0.	0.	0.	0.	0.	2	

Raw Mat'l $ per unit	Fab. Production Rates Next Pd. 1000 units	This Pd. 1000 units	Fab. Labor $ per unit	Fab. # Men Assigned	# Men Hired Or Fired (–)	Fab. Overtime # Hours	
1. 1 0	2 0 0.	2 0 0.	1. 0 0	2 6 0.	0.	0.	3

Purchased Parts $ per unit	Asm. Production Rates Next Pd. 1000 units	This Pd. 1000 units	Asm. Labor $ per unit	Asm. # Men Assigned	# Men Hired Or Fired (–)	Asm. Overtime # Hours	
4 0	2 0 0.	2 0 0.	.7 0	1 8 2.	0.	0.	4

PRODUCT 2

Price Next Period $ per unit	Advertising Budget $1000	Promotion Budget $1000	Prod. Dev. Budget $1000	Mkt. Res. Budget $1000	MR– Price ¢ PU	MR– Adv. $1000	MR– Qual. ¢ PU	MR– P. D. $1000	
2 0. 0 0	8 0.	0.	2 2.	6 5.	1 8 0 0.	0.	9 0 0.	0.	5

Raw Mat'l $ per unit	Fab. Production Rates Next Pd. 1000 units	This Pd. 1000 units	Fab. Labor $ per unit	Fab. # Men Assigned	# Men Hired Or Fired (–)	Fab. Overtime # Hours	
2. 2 0	6 0.	6 0.	2. 4 0	1 3 0.	0.	1 6 0 0 0.	6

Purchased Parts $ per units	Asm. Production Rates Next Pd. 1000 units	This Pd. 1000 units	Asm. Labor $ per unit	Asm. # Men Assigned	# Men Hired Or Fired (–)	Asm. Overtime # Hours	
.6 5	6 0.	6 0.	4. 5 0	2 3 5.	0.	2 6 0 0 0.	7

PRODUCT 3

Price Next Period $ per unit	Advertising Budget $1000	Promotion Budget $1000	Prod. Dev. Budget $1000	Mkt. Res. Budget $1000	MR– Price ¢ PU	MR– Adv. $1000	MR– Qual. ¢ PU	MR– P. D. $1000	
0.	0.	0.	0.	0.	0.	0.	0.	0.	8

Raw Mat'l $ per unit	Fab. Production Rates Next Pd. 1000 units	This Pd. 1000 units	Fab. Labor $ per unit	Fab. # Men Assigned	# Men Hired Or Fired (–)	Fab. Overtime # Hours	
0.	0.	0.	0.	0.	0.	0.	9

Purchased Parts $ per unit	Asm. Production Rates Next Pd. 1000 units	This Pd. 1000 units	Asm. Labor $ per unit	Asm. # Men Assigned	# Men Hired Or Fired (–)	Asm. Overtime # Hours	
0.	0.	0.	0.	0.	0.	0.	10

Marketing Decisions (Lines 1, 4, and 7)

Box 1. Price of product in dollars per unit, for the next period, e.g., $7.70 = 7.70.

Box 2. The advertising budget in thousands of dollars, e.g., $430,000 = 430.

Box 3. The promotion budget in thousands of dollars, e.g., $50,000 = 50.

Box 4. The product development budget in thousands of dollars, e.g., $50,000 = 50.

Box 5. The market research budget in thousands of dollars, e.g., $45,000 = 45.

Box 6A. Price to be tested by market research in cents per unit, e.g., $18.00 = 1800.

Box 6B. Advertising budget to be tested by market research, in $1000.

Box 7A. Quality of product = sum of fabrication and assembly labor budgets plus cost per unit of raw material and purchased parts, to be tested by market research, in cents per unit, e.g., $9.00 = 900.

Box 7B. Product development budget to be tested by market research in $1000.

Fabrication Department Decisions (Lines 2, 5, and 8)

Box 1. Cost per unit of raw material to be purchased, e.g., $1.10 = 1.10.

Box 2. Schedule production rate in 000s of units for the following period. The only purpose of this decision is to order enough raw materials to be available for the first four weeks of the next period, e.g., 240,000 units = 240.

Box 3. Scheduled rate of production in 000s of units for period (per Appendix A actual production may be considerably less) e.g., 265,000 units/period = 265.

Box 4. Labor is scheduled on a per unit basis, e.g., $1.00 = 1.00. The quality level will be met and quantity of units produced will be reduced if there are not enough productive hours available.

Box 5. The *total* number of men assigned to a department of a product. This *includes* men previously assigned *plus or minus* men hired or fired *plus* men transferred from another department and/or product.

Box 6. Number of new employees desired (+) or number of employees to be released (−) from the firm.

Box 7. Total overtime hours desired, e.g., 12,000 = 12,000.

Assembly Department Decisions (Lines 3, 6, and 9)

The format is identical to lines 3, 6, and 9 with purchased parts in place of raw materials.

Exhibit 16 is a copy of the decision form that must be filled out each period for the company as a whole. The form identifies the external financing, building and equipment, cash transfer, and product transfer decisions for the company. It also requires a forecast of earnings per share.

The top line of the decision form is for identification, and complete information here as to corporation number and period is essential to the administration of the simulation.

The succeeding title lines identify the information to be entered in the box directly below the title. Each line will be punched on an IBM card.

External Financial Decisions (Line 1)

Box 1.   Securities purchase decision indicated by a plus (+), sales indicated by a minus (−).

Box 2.   Dividends are paid in multiples of $1000, e.g., $50,000 = 50.

Boxes 3-6. The number of $1000 desired, e.g., $200,000 = 200. Loans are retired automatically.

Forecasted Earnings/Share (Line 2)

Boxes 1-4. Respectively will contain your forecasted earnings per share for each of the next four periods.

Buildings and Equipment Purchases (Line 3)

Boxes 1-6. Respectively will contain the number of $1000 of buildings and equipment purchased of each of the corporation's six plants.

Cash Transfers to and from Divisions (Line 4)

Boxes 1-6. Will indicate the amount of cash to be transferred between each division and headquarters. Cash to be transferred to the division from headquarters will be signified by a plus (+) sign. Cash to be transferred from the division to headquarters will be signified by a minus (−) sign.

Exhibit 16

MANAGEMENT SIMULATION — CORPORATE DECISION FORM

Corporation _____1_____ Period _____2_____ Section _____A_____

External Financial Decisions					
Purchase Securities ($1000)	Dividends ($1000)	90-Day Loans ($100)	One Year Loans ($1000)	Five Year Notes ($1000)	Sell Stock ($1000)
0	875	1500	1500	0	0

Forecasted Earnings Per Share				
This Period	Next Period	Two Periods in Future	Three Periods in Future	
2.00	2.00	2.00	2.00	

Building and Equipment Purchases					
Division 1		Division 2		Division 3	
Northern Plant ($1000)	Southern Plant ($1000)	Northern Plant ($1000)	Southern Plant ($1000)	Northern Plant ($1000)	Southern Plant ($1000)
55.	60.6	65.0	61.3	59.4	63.75

Cash Transfers to and from Divisions			
Division 1	Division 2	Division 3	
0	0	0	

Product Transfers Between Plants

	Plant from			No. of Units (1000)	Plant to			Unit Price
	Product	Plant	Industry		Product	Plant	Industry	
1.	1	2	1		1	2	3	400
2.								
3.								
4.								
5.								

Product Transfers Between Plants (Line 5)

Plant from.   Identify product number, plant (1 for northern and 2 for southern), and industry in which plant is located.

Number of units.   Number of thousands of units to be transferred.

Plant to.   Identify product number, plant (1 for northern and 2 for southern), and industry in which plant is located.

Unit price.   Price transfer will take place at.

Product Statement

EXHIBIT 17 contains a copy of a product statement. Three of these are prepared for each plant every quarter, one for each product line. The following paragraphs identify the significance of key items on the report in the order of their appearance.

REVENUE FROM OUTSIDE SALES = Price times external sales volume for the product concerned.

REVENUE FROM INTERNAL SALES = Transfer price times internal sales volume for product concerned.

COSTS OF GOODS SOLD AT STANDARD COSTS = The sum of the following five items.

FABRICATION LABOR
ASSEMBLY LABOR = Standard unit cost of items sold if there have been no changes. Weighted average standard unit cost of items sold
RAW MATERIALS   during periods when changes are being effected.
PURCHASED PARTS

PURCHASED ITEMS = The original manufacturing cost of all items sold in the period, which were purchased from another plant and the cost of these items to the buying plant.

OVERTIME PREMIUM = Additional cost of overtime hours scheduled at $1.80 per hour for fabrication department and $1.20 per hour for assembly department.

GROSS PROFIT = REVENUE FROM SALES − COST OF GOODS SOLD AT STANDARD COST

FACTORY OVERHEAD

INDIRECT LABOR = $900 × number of idle men + labor efficiency variance.

SUPERVISION = About $160 per worker

MAINTENANCE = Depends on total production volume, about $200 per 1000 units produced for low volumes, $300 per 1000 units for high-volume production + side costs of increasing buildings and equipment capacity.

DEPRECIATION = 2.5 percent of buildings and equipment value allocated on the basis of direct labor hours.

Exhibit 17

```
        I N D U S T R Y   1           P E R I O D  12
  D I V   1 - S O U T H E R N   P L A N T - C O R P O R A T I O N   I
        P R O D U C T   2     I N C O M E   S T A T E M E N T
```

REVENUE FROM OUTSIDE SALES, AT $ 13.50 PER UNIT $ 835421.
REVENUE FROM INTERNAL SALES, AT$ 0.   PER UNIT $ 0.
PRICE NEXT PERIOD $ 13.20 PER UNIT
COST OF GOODS SOLD AT STANDARD COST
    FABRICATION LABOR, AT $ 1.93 PER UNIT   119436.
    ASSEMBLY LABOR,   AT $ 2.66 PER UNIT   164741.
    RAW MATERIALS,   AT $ 1.70 PER UNIT   105299.
    PURCHASED PARTS,   AT $ 0.53 PER UNIT   32867.
    PURCHASED ITEMS(MFG COST   0.)   0.
    OVERTIME PREMIUM   0.   422343.
GROSS PROFIT   413078.

FACTORY OVERHEAD
    INDIRECT LABOR   648.
    SUPERVISION   45234.
    MAINTENANCE   10071.
    DEPRECIATION   16337.   72289.

MARKETING AND ADMINISTRATIVE EXPENSES
    ADVERTISING   110000.
    PROMOTION   35000.
    COMMISSIONS AND SALESMENS EXPENSE   50771.
    WAREHOUSE AND SHIPPING   10011.
    PRODUCT DEVELOPMENT   39000.
    MARKET RESEARCH   0.
    ADMINISTRATIVE   14044.   258826.
OPERATING PROFIT $ 81963.

P R O D U C T I O N

	FABRICATION DEPT.	ASSEMBLY DEPT.
PRODUCTION VOLUME, UNITS	48732.	48811.
W.I.P. INVENTORY, UNITS	12183.	8166.
NUMBER OF MEN HIRED OR FIRED	0.	0.
NUMBER OF MEN BUDGETED	111.	158.
NUMBER OF MEN WORKING	111.	158.
NUMBER OF HOURS AVAILABLE	55500.	78667.
PERCENT HOURS UTILIZED	100.	100.
NUMBER OF HOURS OVERTIME	0.	0.

I N V E N T O R I E S

RAW MATERIALS AT $ 1.80 PER UNIT, 16333. UNITS
PURCHASED PARTS AT $ 0.55 PER UNIT, 24689. UNITS
FABRICATED PARTS AT $ 3.85 AVERAGE PER UNIT   8313. UNITS
FINISHED GOODS, IN UNITS
    BEGINNING   31141.
    PRODUCTION   49811.
    UNITS TRANSFERRED IN   0.
    LESS GOODS IN TRANSIT   0.
    GOODS AVAILABLE   80952.
    ORDERS RECEIVED FROM OUTSIDE CUSTOMERS   61883.
    SALES LOST FROM OUTSIDE CUSTOMERS   0.
    INTERNAL SALES VOLUME   0.
    SALES VOLUME   61883.
    ENDING, AT $ 7.02 AVERAGE COST PER UNIT   19069.

    SHARE OF INDUSTRY UNIT SALES VOLUME, PERCENT   2.

MARKETING AND ADMINISTRATIVE EXPENSE

ADVERTISING, PROMOTION, PRODUCT DEVELOPMENT,
AND MARKET RESEARCH = Budgets (i.e., entries on decision form prepared in period)

COMMISSIONS AND
SALESMEN'S EXPENSES = Commision rate of 5 percent of sales dollars + about $.15 per unit sold.

WAREHOUSE AND SHIPPING = $.03 per unit of total work in process and fabricated parts inventories on hand plus $.03 per unit of finished goods inventory plus one percent of the finished goods inventory evaluation plus $.10 per unit sold plus one and a half percent of the value of raw material and purchase parts inventories on hand.

ADMINISTRATIVE = One administrator for about every 50,000 units produced in each department (i.e., Product 1, assembly, Product 1, fabrication, and so forth) at about $4000 per period + one top executive for each million dollars worth of buildings and equipment at an average salary of about $25,000 per year allocated to products on the basis of direct labor hours plus costs associated with hiring and firing men.

OPERATING PROFIT = GROSS PROFIT − FACTORY OVERHEAD − MARKETING AND ADMINISTRATIVE EXPENSES

PRODUCTION

This report covers both fabrication and assembly departments separately.

PRODUCTION VOLUME, UNITS = Number of units that enter that department during period.

W.I.P. INVENTORY, UNIT = Number of units in process at end of period, i.e., fabrication department, three weeks' amount production, assembly department, two weeks' amount.

NUMBER OF MEN BUDGETED = Actual entries made on decision form for period.

NUMBER OF MEN WORKING = Actual number of men working in department in period. This number will be smaller than the number of men budgeted only when you try to assign more workers than you have available in your workforce.

NUMBER OF HOURS AVAILABLE = 500 hours per man previously assigned and less for men transferred or hired plus number of hours overtime.

PERCENT HOURS UTILIZED $\qquad$ = An indicator of the efficiency of the labor force

$$= \frac{\text{number of standard hours needed for period's production}}{\text{NUMBER OF HOURS AVAILABLE}}$$

INVENTORIES

FINISHED GOODS, PRODUCTION = Number of units completed by assembly department.

UNITS TRANSFERRED IN = Number of units received from another plant in the period.

GOODS IN TRANSIT = Number of units that have been irrevocably committed for sale to another plant.

SHARE OF INDUSTRY SALES VOLUME, PERCENT = Percent of total industry unit sales generated by this product.

MARKET RESEARCH

SALES = Number of units.

Plant Income Statement

EXHIBIT 18 (p. 80) is a copy of the income statement prepared for each plant every period. This report summarizes income figures, plant status, and the business index.

INCOME STATEMENT = This simply totals the individual product reports.

PLANT REPORT = Directly below the income statement is a plant report summarizing the value of buildings and equipment during the period following the date of the report. You will want to use this in determining the maximum total labor force for next period, i.e., one man per $2500 plant. The TOTAL NUMBER OF EMPLOYEES for this period is also shown. This should be the total of men assigned to each department plus idle men, if any. The total number of men in the IDLE LABOR POOL is identified separately.

GAIN FROM NEW INVESTMENT = Buildings and equipment purchase decisions last period.

Plant Balance Sheet and Cash Flow Statement

EXHIBIT 19 (p. 81) contains copies of the plant balance sheet and cash flow statement that are prepared each period. The following paragraphs identify how each of the items on the report is calculated.

BALANCE SHEET

CASH = Former value of same item plus net cash inflow for the period (which of course represents a reduction when negative).

ACCOUNTS RECEIVABLE = Approximately 30 percent of sales of current period.

INVENTORIES = The sum of the inventory valuation for individual products.

CURRENT ASSETS = The sum of the four items just listed.

BUILDINGS AND EQUIPMENT, NET = The end-of-period value of buildings and equipment − depreciation. This is the value the maximum number of efficient employees is dependent upon for the next period.

TOTAL ASSETS = current assets + buildings and equipment, net.

ACCOUNTS PAYABLE = About thirty days' worth of raw material and purchased parts purchases and one third of the marketing budget.

CASH FLOW

Those items that may be difficult to understand are explained as follows.

CASH SALES = Cash sales made during period to outside customers.

CASH FROM ACCOUNTS RECEIVABLE = Opening accounts receivable, normally about 30 percent of sales of prior period.

CASH FROM DIVISION = Cash supplied by division to sustain plant's operations. It is automatically provided in accounts necessary to pay all due bills and sustain the plant's minimum cash balance.

TOTAL CASH EXPENDITURE = MARKETING AND ADMINISTRATIVE EXPENSES + SUPERVISION AND MAINTENANCE COSTS + $900 X total number of men + TOTAL COST OF OVERTIME + opening accounts payable − closing accounts payable + raw material and purchased parts purchases.

CASH PAYMENTS TO INTERDIVISIONAL SALES = Cash payment for goods purchased from other corporation divisions.

CASH TO DIVISION = All excess cash beyond minimum cash balance is automatically remitted to division at end of period.

Industry Report

EXHIBIT 20 (p. 82) contains a copy of the plant's industry report which is prepared each period.

Each plant in an industry receives the identical industry report which presents gross statistics on all competitors in an industry. The data presented under the titles PROFIT AND LOSS and FINANCIAL CONDITION are expressed in $1000 and are accurate. The data under individual products, with the exception of PRICE NEXT PER are *not* accurate but have been randomized. This gives you an indication of what other plants are doing but prevents the immediate identifying of shifts in tactics. In most instances these figures are within 20 percent of their actual values. PRICE and DIRECT CPU are in dollars; ADVERTISING sales promotion, and PRODUCT DEVELOP budgets are in $100, and sales units are in 1000s. Products 1, 2, and 3 are listed from left to right.

Divisional Income Statement

EXHIBIT 21 (p. 83) is a copy of the income statement prepared for each division each period. This statement is a combination of the plant income statements. The figure in this statement should coincide exactly with the sum of the plant figures except as follows:

1. TOTAL SALES REVENUE figures will differ (lower) if there have been any intradivisional period sales (which will be eliminated in the consolidation).

2. COSTS OF GOODS SOLD figures will differ if

   a. There have been any intradivisional sales in the period,

   b. Any merchandise is sold to customers which was moved on an intradivisional transfer (either this period or in a previous period).

Divisional Balance Sheet and Cash Flow Statement

EXHIBIT 22 (p. 84) is a copy of the balance sheet and cash flow statement prepared for each division every period. This statement is a consolidation of the plant balance sheet. The figures in this statement should coincide exactly with the sum of the plant balance sheet except as follows:

1. Cash surplus at divisional level is now information that cannot be found in plant statements.

2. Goods for intracompany sales inventory figure is altered to eliminate any profits (or losses) from intradivisional sales.

Corporation Income Statement, Plant Report

EXHIBIT 23 (p. 85) is a copy of the company's income statement which is prepared each period. At the bottom of the statement is a summary of the corporation's buildings and equipment status and the same business index figures as on the plant and divisional income statements.

Down through OPERATING PROFIT, this simply totals the individual division income statements (eliminating interdivisional sales and profits made thereon). Note that items that have been transferred, have their costs incorporated in the line int transfers—orig cost at the time of sale and are not included in the fabrication labor, assembly labor, raw materials, and purchased parts figures. The other entries are determined as follows:

INTEREST EXPENSE = FINANCIAL INTEREST

BANK CHARGES − EMERGENCY CASH = One percent of amount of emergency loans made to division at end of period to maintain plant minimum cash balances.

SECURITY INCOME is earned and entered at the rate of one percent per period, on the value of securities held throughout each period.

TAXABLE INCOME = OPERATING PROFIT + SECURITY INCOME − INTEREST EXPENSE

INCOME TAX = 52 percent of taxable income. There is an immediate tax rebate in case of loss up to the amount of taxes your firm has paid.

NET INCOME = TAXABLE INCOME − INCOME TAX

The plant report is simply a combination of the buildings and equipment data on the divisional reports.

Corporation Balance Sheet and Cash Flow Statement

EXHIBIT 24 (p. 86) contains a copy of the company's balance sheet which is prepared each period. Underneath the balance sheet are a set of financial ratios and a cash flow statement. The following paragraphs identify how each of the items in the report is calculated.

BALANCE SHEET

CASH HEADQUARTERS

CASH DIVISIONAL = Former value of same item plus net cash inflow for the period (which, of course, represents a reduction when negative). (Sum of cash balances appearing on division balance sheets).

SECURITIES = Former value of same item plus purchase (or minus sale) of securities during the period concerned.

ACCOUNTS RECEIVABLE = Approximately 30 percent of sales of current period. (Sum of accounts receivables on divisional balance sheets.)

INVENTORIES = The sum of the inventory valuation for individual products. (Will differ from total of inventories on divisional balance sheets if profits (or losses) on interdivisional sales have to be backed out.)

CURRENT ASSETS = The sum of the four items just listed.

BUILDINGS AND EQUIPMENT, NET = The end-of-period value of plant minus depreciation. (Sum of buildings and equipment of divisional balance sheets.) This is the value the maximum number of efficient employees is dependent upon the next period.

TOTAL ASSETS = CURRENT ASSETS + BUILDINGS AND EQUIPMENT, NET

ACCOUNTS PAYABLE = About thirty days' worth of raw material and purchased parts purchases and one third of the advertising budget. (Sum of accounts payable on divisional balance sheets.)

NOTES PAYABLE = Total of all loans and notes due within one year, including portion of five-year notes due within one year.

TAXES = Amount of taxes owed. In case of a loss, there is an immediate rebate, if tax credits exist, which will show under the cash flow receipts. In case of a profit, the tax owed will appear here to be paid next period.

CURRENT LIABILITIES = The sum of the three items just listed.

LONG-TERM DEBT = Amount of five-year notes not due within one year.

COMMON STOCK = Number of shares and total par value.

SURPLUS = Retained earnings.

TOTAL LIABILITIES AND EQUITY = CURRENT LIABILITIES plus the three items just listed.

Financial ratios

1. TOTAL LIABILITIES TO TOTAL ASSETS

$$= \frac{\text{CURRENT LIABILITiES} + \text{LONG-TERM DEBT}}{\text{TOTAL ASSETS}}$$

2. LONG-TERM DEBT TO TOTAL ASSETS = self-explanatory.

3. QUICK RATIO

$$= \frac{\text{cash} + \text{securities} + \text{accounts receivable}}{\text{current liabilities}}$$

4. CURRENT RATIO

$$= \frac{\text{current assets}}{\text{current liabilities}}$$

5. FIXED CHARBE COVERAGE

$$0 \ \frac{\text{average* profit before taxes} + \text{depreciation}}{\frac{\text{sinking fund}}{(1 - \text{tax rate})} + \text{interest}}$$

STOCK PRICE = dollars per share.

CASH FLOW

Most entries are self-explanatory. Note the following, however.

CASH FROM ACCOUNTS RECEIVABLE = Opening accounts receivable, usually about 30 percent of sales of prior period.

INCOME FROM SECURITIES = One percent of value of securities held or sold this period.

CASH FROM SECURITIES, NOTES and STOCK appears only when applicable.

TOTAL CASH EXPENDITURES = MARKETING AND ADMINISTRATIVE EXPENSES + INTEREST + SUPERVISION AND MAINTENANCE COSTS + $900 × total number of men + total cost of overtime + opening accounts payable − closing accounts payable + raw material and purchased parts purchases.

REPAYMENT OF FIVE-YEAR NOTE = Amount of five-year note repaid during the period.

*This period and last three periods.

Divisional Report

EXHIBIT 25 (p. 87) contains a summary of the information on the divisional and plant reports (i.e., income statement, balance sheet, and product line statement) for use by the corporate staff. This report is prepared each period. Most items, with the exception of those in the cash flow statement, are self-explanatory.

OPERATIONS	=	CASH SALES + collection of accounts receivable — cash expense.
CORPORATION	=	Cash given to or taken from division at beginning of period by headquarters.
DSTRSS CASH	=	Cash given to division at end of period by headquarters because cash level below provided minimum.
PLANT PUR	=	Cash outlays for plant purchase during period.
CASH DECREASE, CASH INCREASE	=	Net change in the division's cash balance over the course of the period.

PRODUCT LINE REPORT

This report presents summary data on the performance of each of the division's product lines. The data on external sales is taken directly from Exhibit 17 (p. 71). The entries are interpreted as follows:

PRICE	=	Price to outside customers during period.
C.P.U.	=	Cost/unit of items sold to outside customers during period.
ADVERTISING	=	Total advertising expenditures supporting product during period.
PROD DEV	=	Total product development expenditures supporting product during period.
OPER PROF	=	Product's operating profit net of the sales revenue and direct manufacturing costs (i.e., fabrication, labor, assembly labor, raw materials, and purchased parts) of items sold internally.

The internal sales entries refer to items sold to other plants during the period (i.e., physically transferred out of the selling plant).

AV. PRICE	=	Average sales prices of units sold internally.
SLS UNITS	=	Total number of units sold internally.
ORDER PROF	=	Total number of units sold internally multiplied by the difference between the price and cost/unit of these units.

The entries under MFG. STAT. may be interpreted as follows:

PROD VOL	=	Total unit output (in 000s) from the product's assembly department during the period.

FGD INV = Number of units (in 000s) in finished goods inventory at the end of the period.

NR MEN = Total number of men working in the product's fabrication and assembly departments during period.

HRS OVTM = Total number of hours of overtime (in 000s) in the product's fabrication and assembly departments during period.

PERCENT UTIL = Average efficiency of workers in the product's fabrication and assembly departments during period.

Exhibit 18

M A N A G E M E N T   S I M U L A T I O N

I N D U S T R Y   1 - C O R P O R A T I O N   1 - D I V I S I O N   1

I N C O M E   S T A T E M E N T   P E R I O D   12

S O U T H E R N   P L A N T

```
TOTAL SALES REVENUE                                    $    2912434.

COST OF GOODS SOLD
     FABRICATION LABOR                        395946.
     ASSEMBLY LABOR                           473920.
     RAW MATERIALS                            379409.
     PURCHASED PARTS                          124071.
     PURCHASED ITEMS(MFG COST 103336.)        105000.
     OVERTIME PREMIUM                              0.        1478346.

  G R O S S   P R O F I T                                   1434088.

FACTORY OVERHEAD
     INDIRECT LABOR                              672.
     SUPERVISION                              150780.
     MAINTENANCE                               55816.
     DEPRECIATION                              53538.         260805.

MARKETING AND ADMINISTRATIVE EXPENSES
     ADVERTISING                              450000.
     PROMOTION                                 60000.
     COMMISSIONS AND SALESMENS EXPENSE        192121.
     WAREHOUSE AND SHIPPING                    47054.
     MARKET RESEARCH                              0.
     PRODUCT DEVELOPMENT                      120000.
     ADMINISTRATIVE                            63995.         933170.

  N E T   I N C O M E                                  $     240113.


        B U I L D I N G S   A N D   E Q U I P M E N T   R E P O R T
BUILD/EQUIP CAPACITY, PERIOD   13       $   2141980.
LOSS FROM DEPRECIATION                       53549.
GAIN FROM NEW INVESTMENT                         0.
BUILD/EQUIP CAPACITY, PERIOD   14       $   2088430.
TOTAL NUMBER OF EMPLOYEES                      880.
```

B U S I N E S S   I N D E X   (SEASONALLY ADJUSTED)

PERIODS 9 TO 12 (ACTUAL)	675	678	685	692
PERIODS 13 TO 16 (ESTIMATED)	711	721	733	748
PERIODS 17 TO 20 (ESTIMATED)	731	771	759	780

Exhibit 19

```
B A L A N C E   S H E E T      P E R I O D  12

I N D U S T R Y    1 - C O R P O R A T I O N    1 - D I V I S I O N    1

S O U T H E R N   P L A N T
```

CASH		119346.
ACCOUNTS RECEIVABLE		961199.
INVENTORIES		
RAW MATERIALS	118584.	
PURCHASED PARTS	60405.	
WORK IN PROCESS	389624.	
FABRICATED PARTS	133468.	
FINISHED GOODS	484359.	
GOODS FOR INTRACOMPANY SALES	-0.	1186440.
CURRENT ASSETS		2266985.
BUILDINGS AND EQUIPMENT, NET		2141980.
T O T A L A S S E T S		4408965.
ACCCUNTS PAYABLE		290081.
DIFFERENCE BETWEEN TOTAL ASSETS AND TOTAL LIABILITIES		4118884.

```
              C A S H   F L O W
```

CASH SALES	1951235.
CASH FROM INTERDIVISIONAL SALES	0.
CASH FROM ACCOUNTS RECEIVABLE	1012948.
CASH FROM DIVISION	0.
T O T A L R E C E I P T S	2964183.
TOTAL CASH EXPENDITURES	2386919.
CASH PAYMENTS TO INTERDIVISIONAL SALES	105000.
CAPITAL EXPENDITURES, BUILDINGS AND EQUIPMENT	54000.
CASH TO DIVISION	418968.
T O T A L D I S B U R S E M E N T S	2964887.
N E T C A S H I N F L O W	-704.

Exhibit 20

```
I N D U S T R Y   R E P O R T - I N D U S T R Y   1 - P E R I O D   12
C O R P O R A T I O N   1 - D I V I S I O N   1
         PROFIT AND LOSS                    FINANCIAL CONDITION
      SALES RVNUE      6014.        CASH                  913.
      TOT EXPENSE      5398.        INVENTORY            2467.
      OPER PROFIT       616.        BLDG.-EQUIP-NO.      2300.
                                    BLDG.-EQUIP-SO.      2142.
                                    CUR LIAB              590.

  INDIVIDUAL PRODUCTS       NORTHERN PLANT              SOUTHERN PLANT
      PRICE            9.70     5.50    30.00  *      7.20    13.50    18.00
      ADVT AND PROM  158.95   295.96    34.95  *    270.84   146.71   103.97
      PROD DEVEL      83.25    63.57     5.14  *     58.98    39.72    21.82
      DIRECT CPU       4.64     2.58    15.81  *      3.46     7.15    10.68
      SLS UNITS,     140.57   340.58     4.68  *    207.91    59.94    30.96

      PRICE NEXT PER   9.50     5.45    25.00  *      7.04    13.20    17.10
**********************************************************************

C O R P O R A T I O N   3 - D I V I S I O N   2
         PROFIT AND LOSS                    FINANCIAL CONDITION
      SALES RVNUE      8023.        CASH                 1022.
      TOT EXPENSE      7402.        INVENTORY            3321.
      OPER PROFIT       620.        BLDG.-EQUIP-NO.      3038.
                                    BLDG.-EQUIP-SO.      3294.
                                    CUR LIAB              798.

  INDIVIDUAL PRODUCTS       NORTHERN PLANT              SOUTHERN PLANT
      PRICE            6.50    15.50     7.95  *      4.20    11.25    22.00
      ADVT AND PROM  375.98   120.17   361.37  *    276.81   187.78    98.72
      PROD DEVEL      52.16    30.52    30.31  *     59.17    42.02    20.21
      DIRECT CPU       2.92     8.35     4.74  *      2.16     6.67    11.30
      SLS UNITS,     222.96    41.15   261.50  *    407.56   149.15    24.85

      PRICE NEXT PER   6.50    15.50     8.50  *      4.20    11.25    21.50
**********************************************************************

C O R P O R A T I O N   5 - D I V I S I O N   3
         PROFIT AND LOSS                    FINANCIAL CONDITION
      SALES RVNUE      8649.        CASH                 1321.
      TOT EXPENSE      7660.        INVENTORY            4479.
      OPER PROFIT       989.        BLDG.-EQUIP-NO.      2995.
                                    BLDG.-EQUIP-SO.      3206.
                                    CUR LIAB              774.

  INDIVIDUAL PRODUCTS       NORTHERN PLANT              SOUTHERN PLANT
      PRICE           15.99     5.35     4.99  *     12.25     5.69    10.25
      ADVT AND PROM  169.52     0.     379.35  *    259.46   416.16   169.57
      PROD DEVEL      53.67     0.      66.08  *     50.04    87.51    81.36
      DIRECT CPU       8.36     2.50     2.25  *      6.51     2.87     4.59
      SLS UNITS,      69.46    24.12   403.38  *    120.91   439.88   147.02

      PRICE NEXT PER  15.99     5.35     4.75  *     12.25     5.79    10.25
**********************************************************************
```

Exhibit 21

M A N A G E M E N T   S I M U L A T I O N

I N D U S T R Y   1 — C O R P O R A T I O N   1 — D I V I S I O N   1

I N C O M E   S T A T E M E N T   P E R I O D   12

TOTAL SALES REVENUE		$ 6109896.
COST OF GOODS SOLD		
FABRICATION LABOR	857120.	
ASSEMBLY LABOR	906668.	
RAW MATERIALS	855590.	
PURCHASED PARTS	309103.	
PURCHASED ITEMS	105000.	
OVERTIME PREMIUM	0.	3033481.
G R O S S P R O F I T		3076415.
FACTORY OVERHEAD		
INDIRECT LABOR	3506.	
SUPERVISION	283969.	
MAINTENANCE	142426.	
DEPRECIATION	112503.	542404.
MARKETING AND ADMINISTRATIVE EXPENSES		
ADVERTISING	820000.	
PROMOTION	174000.	
COMMISSIONS AND SALESMENS EXPENSE	399694.	
WAREHOUSE AND SHIPPING	112643.	
MARKET RESEARCH	0.	
PRODUCT DEVELOPMENT	275000.	
ADMINISTRATIVE	136384.	1917721.
N E T I N C O M E		$ 616291.

S O U T H E R N   B U I L D / E Q U I P   R E P O R T

BUILD/EQUIP CAPACITY, PERIOD 13	$	2141980.
LOSS FROM DEPRECIATION		53549.
GAIN FROM NEW INVESTMENT		0.
BUILD/EQUIP CAPACITY, PERIOD 14	$	2088430.
TOTAL NUMBER OF EMPLOYEES		880.

N O R T H E R N   B U I L D / E Q U I P   R E P O R T

BUILD/EQUIP CAPACITY, PERIOD 13	$	2299631.
LOSS FROM DEPRECIATION		57491.
GAIN FROM NEW INVESTMENT		0.
BUILD/EQUIP CAPACITY, PERIOD 14	$	2242140.
TOTAL NUMBER OF EMPLOYEES		789.

B U S I N E S S   I N D E X (SEASONALLY ADJUSTED)

PERIODS 9 TO 12 (ACTUAL)	675	678	685	692
PERIODS 13 TO 16 (ESTIMATED)	711	721	733	748
PERIODS 17 TO 20 (ESTIMATED)	731	771	759	760

Exhibit 22

B A L A N C E   S H E E T   P E R I O D   12

I N D U S T R Y   1 - C O R P O R A T I O N   1 - D I V I S I O N   1

```
CASH TO SUPPORT MINIMUM NEEDS OF PLANTS                    242494.
CASH SURPLUS AT DIVISIONAL LEVEL                           670539.
ACCOUNTS RECEIVABLE                                       1984784.
INVENTORIES
   RAW MATERIALS                        259485.
   PURCHASED PARTS                      137181.
   WORK IN PROCESS                      803537.
   FABRICATED PARTS                     211484.
   FINISHED GOODS                      1054900.
   GOODS FOR INTRACOMPANY SALES              0.
                                                          2466587.
CURRENT ASSETS                                            5364404.
BUILDINGS AND EQUIPMENT, NET                              4441610.

T O T A L   A S S E T S                                   9806014.

ACCOUNTS PAYABLE                                           590019.

DIFFERENCE BETWEEN TOTAL ASSETS AND TOTAL LIABILITIES     9215996.
```

```
          C A S H   F L O W
CASH SALES                                               4029112.
CASH FROM INTERDIVISIONAL SALES                            96000.
CASH FROM ACCOUNTS RECEIVABLE                            2126052.
CASH FROM CORPORATION                                          0.
EMERGENCY CASH FROM CORP                                       0.

T O T A L   R E C E I P T S                              6251164.

TOTAL CASH EXPENDITURES                                  4849889.
CASH PAYMENTS TO INTERDIVISIONAL SALES                    105000.
CAPITAL EXPENDITURES, BUILDINGS AND EQUIPMENT              54000.
CASH TO CORPORATION                                      1000000.
T O T A L   D I S B U R S E M E N T S                    6008889.

N E T   C A S H   I N F L O W                             242275.
```

Exhibit 23

M A N A G E M E N T   S I M U L A T I O N

C O R P O R A T I O N   1

I N C O M E   S T A T E M E N T   P E R I O D   12

TOTAL SALES REVENUE $ 18308180.

COST OF GOODS SOLD
FABRICATION LABOR	2654234.	
ASSEMBLY LABOR	2600842.	
RAW MATERIALS	2694778.	
PURCHASED PARTS	956370.	
OVERTIME PREMIUM	0.	
INT TRANSFERS — ORIG COST	163140.	9069364.

G R O S S   P R O F I T 9238816.

FACTORY OVERHEAD
INDIRECT LABOR	7502.	
SUPERVISION	861959.	
MAINTENANCE	447743.	
DEPRECIATION	355788.	1672992.

MARKETING AND ADMINISTRATIVE EXPENSES
ADVERTISING	2557000.	
PROMOTION	431000.	
COMMISSIONS AND SALESMENS EXPENSE	1240909.	
WAREHOUSE AND SHIPPING	357988.	
MARKET RESEARCH	0.	
PRODUCT DEVELOPMENT	802000.	
ADMINISTRATIVE	452137.	5832283.

OPERATING PROFIT 1733540.

INTEREST EXPENSE	90000.
BANK CHARGES—EMERGENCY CASH	0.
SECURITY INCOME	3000.
TAXABLE INCOME	1646540.
INCOME TAX	856201.

N E T   I N C O M E $ 790339.

P L A N T   R E P O R T

PLANT CAPACITY, PERIOD 13	$ 13992725.
LOSS FROM DEPRECIATION	349818.
GAIN FROM NEW INVESTMENT	0.
PLANT CAPACITY, PERIOD 14	$ 13642907.

TOTAL NUMBER OF EMPLOYEES 5061.

B U S I N E S S   I N D E X (SEASONALLY ADJUSTED)

PERIODS 9 TO 12 (ACTUAL)	675	678	685	692
PERIODS 13 TO 16 (ESTIMATED)	711	721	733	748
PERIODS 17 TO 20 (ESTIMATED)	731	771	759	760

85

Exhibit 24

```
                      C O R P O R A T I O N    1
               B A L A N C E   S H E E T      P E R I O D   12
   CASH (HEADQUARTERS)                                                    50000.
   CASH (DIVISIONAL)                                                    2932960.
   SECURITIES                                                           1133012.
   ACCOUNTS RECEIVABLE                                                  6042304.
   INVENTORIES
       RAW MATERIALS                       791254.
       PURCHASED PARTS                     422887.
       WORK IN PROCESS                    2465221.
       FABRICATED PARTS                    726929.
       FINISHED GOODS                     4022967.                      8429258.
   CURRENT ASSETS                                                      18587534.
   BLDG. AND EQUIPMENT, NET                                            13992725.

   T O T A L   A S S E T S                                             32580259.

   ACCOUNTS PAYABLE                                                     1839624.
   NOTES PAYABLE                                                        4500000.
   TAXES                                                                 856201.
   CURRENT LIABILITIES                                                  7195825.
   LONG TERM DEBT                                                             0.
   COMMON STOCK                  3000000. SHARES                       14252500.
   SURPLUS                                                             11131934.

   T O T A L   L I A B I L I T I E S   A N D   E Q U I T Y             32580259.
```

```
   TOTAL LIAB TO     LONG TERM DEBT    QUICK     CURRENT    FIXED CHARGES
   TOTAL ASSETS      TO TOTAL ASSETS   RATIO     RATIO      COVERAGE
      22 0/0             0 0/0          1.41      2.58        15.07
```

STOCK PRICE $ 10

```
               C A S H   F L O W
   CASH SALES                                                          12505176.
   CASH FROM ACCOUNTS RECEIVABLE                                        6496307.
   INCOME FROM SECURITIES                                                  3000.

   T O T A L   R E C E I P T S                                         19004483.

   TOTAL CASH EXPENDITURES (INCL INTEREST)                             15139769.
   TAXES PAID                                                           1094091.
   SECURITIES PURCHASED                                                  833012.
   CAPITAL EXPENDITURES, PLANT                                           117000.
   DIVIDENDS PAID                                                       1200000.
   REPAYMENT OF 90 DAY LOANS                                                  0.
   REPAYMENT OF ONE YEAR LOAN                                                 0.
   REPAYMENT OF FIVE YEAR NOTE                                                0.

   T O T A L   D I S B U R S E M E N T S                               18383872.

   N E T   C A S H   I N F L O W                                         620611.
```

Exhibit 25

CORPORATION 1 - PERIOD12 - DIVISIONAL REPORT

CIVISION 1 (LOCATED IN INDUSTRY 1)

```
        BALANCE SHEET                    CASH FLOW STATEMENT
     ASSETS           LIAB/N.W.        SCURCES           APPLICATIONS
CASH          913. ACCT PAY     590. OPERATICNS 1296.  CPERATICNS      0.
ACCTS REC    1985.                    DSTRSS CASH   0.  B-ECP PUR      54.
INVENTCRY    2467.                    CCRPCRATICN   0.  CORPORATION 1C00.
BLDG-EQUP-N  2300.                    CSH DECREASE  0.  CSH INCREASEI242.
BLDG-EQUP-S  2142. ASSET-LIAB   9216.  TCTAL     2296.   TOTAL     2296.
   TCTAL     9806.   TOTAL      9806.
```

```
       INCOME STATEMENT
SALES                   6110.
   LESS C.G.S.          3033.

GROSS PROFIT            3076.
EXPENSES
   FAC OHD       542.
   M AND A      1918.   2460.
OPER PRCF                616.
```

PRODUCT LINE REPORT

	NORTHERN PLANT			SOUTHERN PLANT		
	1	2	3	1	2	3
EXTERNAL SALES						
PRICE	9.70	5.50	30.00	7.20	13.50	18.00
C.P.U.	4.45	2.62	15.58	3.53	6.82	10.06
SLS UNITS	130.	308.	5.	210.	62.	31.
ADVERTISNG	160.	290.	34.	265.	145.	100.
PROC DEV	85.	65.	5.	58.	39.	23.
OPER PRCF	175.	176.	23.	134.	82.	24.
INTERNAL SALES						
AV PRICE	0.	0.	16.00	0.	0.	0.
SLS UNITS	0.	0.	6.	0.	0.	0.
OPER PRCF	0.	0.	3.	0.	0.	0.
MFG STAT						
PROC VOL	140.	249.	-0.	187.	50.	25.
FGD INV	33.	108.	8.	64.	19.	12.
NR MEN	420.	369.	0.	411.	269.	200.
HRS OVTM	0.	0.	0.	0.	0.	0.
O/O UTIL	99.	100.	0.	100.	100.	100.

Appendix A

Determination of Production Output

Labor Efficiency Buildup

To enable accurate planning of production schedules, Exhibit A1 (p.89) is provided to show the rate of increase in the efficiency of new men. The chart shows the number of standard hours (to the nearest half hour) of production available in any given week from one hired or transferred man. For example, one newly hired man will provide 4 standard production hours in the first week of the quarter and will gradually work up to full efficiency by the end of the quarter, or approximately 41 1/2 hours a week (500 hours per quarter divided by 12.

Exhibit A1 (p.89) can be used to determine the maximum number of units that enter a department each week. To do this, the following steps must be taken:

1. The number of men in each of the six labor categories indicated in Exhibit A1 must be determined.

2. The number of men in each category is then multiplied by the appropriate standard production hours figure from Exhibit A1. This will give the number of hours available in each category.

3. The hours available from step 2 can then be converted into a unit production rate by using the departmental labor cost per unit figure on the decision sheet and by recognizing that workers are being paid $1.80 per hour. These numbers

Exhibit A1

Standard Production Hours of Output Obtained from Each Man Each Week in a Quarter

Week	1	2	3	4	5	6	7	8	9	10	11	12
Newly hired men	4.0	7.5	11.0	14.5	18.0	21.0	24.5	28.0	32.5	35.0	38.0	41.5
Men transferred across products in same department	31.0	33.5	35.5	37.5	39.5	41.5	41.5	41.5	41.5	41.5	41.5	41.5
Men transferred across departments in same product	25.0	37.5	30.0	32.0	34.5	37.0	39.0	41.5	41.5	41.5	41.5	41.5
Men transferred across both departments and products	16.5	19.5	22.0	25.0	28.0	30.5	33.5	36.0	39.0	41.5	41.5	41.5
Idle men assigned to work	31.0	33.5	37.5	39.5	41.5	41.5	41.5	41.5	41.5	41.5	41.5	41.5
Experienced men	41.5	41.5	41.5	41.5	41.5	41.5	41.5	41.5	41.5	41.5	41.5	41.5

when added will indicate the amount of production in units that can enter a department each week.

These steps may be summarized by the following formula:

$$\begin{matrix} \text{Number of units} \\ \text{entering department} \\ \text{in week } w \end{matrix} = \frac{\$1.80}{\text{labor cost per unit}} \times \sum_{n-1}^{6} M_n \times H_{n,w}$$

M_n = Number of workers in category n

$H_{n,w}$ = Number of standard hours of production that a worker in category n can produce in week w.

Exhibit A2 (p.91) shows a worksheet that has been filled out using the preceding three steps and the following data:

1. Three men have been hired.

2. Three men have been transferred from another product in the same department.

3. Two men have been transferred from another department in the same product.

4. One man has been transferred from another department and another product.

5. One idle man has been put to work.

6. Twenty-two men are experienced, having worked in this department and on this product last period.

7. The labor cost per unit in this department is $.90.

For example, to find the maximum number of units entering a department that can be handled by newly hired workers in week 1, multiply number of men (3) times hours per man (4) times $1.80 and divide by the labor cost per unit ($.90). Thus, three newly hired men will allow up to twenty-four units to be introduced during the first week of a quarter's production. Altogether the hired, transferred, and experienced men in this department will permit 2231 units to be introduced into the department during the first week. This worksheet can thus be used to determine the production rate that can be obtained each week from the work force in a department.

Production Processing Delays

A second factor to be considered in the planning of finished goods production is the time delay associated with changing work-in-process inventory levels to support the new production rate. Exhibit A3 (p. 92) contains a sample problem to show how many units there are in each of the inventories each week. The following data was used for this problem.

Exhibit A2

WORKSHEET FOR PRODUCT X , DEPT. y

(All values in units)

	1	2	3	4	5	6	7	8	9	10	11	12
1. Week	1	2	3	4	5	6	7	8	9	10	11	12
2. Hired	24	45	66	87	108	126	147	168	189	210	228	249
3. Different products	186	201	213	225	237	249	249	249	249	249	249	249
4. Different depts.	100	110	120	128	138	148	156	166	166	166	166	166
5. Across both	33	39	44	50	56	61	67	72	78	83	83	83
6. Idle men	62	67	75	79	83	83	83	83	83	83	83	83
7. Experienced men	1826	1826	1826	1826	1826	1826	1826	1826	1826	1826	1826	1826
8. Weekly production rate (add lines 2–7)	2231	2288	2344	2395	2448	2493	2528	2564	2591	2617	2635	2656
9. Amount of desired rate increase than can be implemented each week												
10. Total possible production rate (line 9 + previous period's weekly rate)												
11. Actual production rate per week (line 8 or 10, whichever is less)												

Exhibit A3

PRODUCTION DELAYS AND INVENTORIES

Week	Raw Materials Inventory	First Week Fabrication	Second Week Fabrication	Third Week Fabrication	Fabricated Parts Inventory	Purchased Parts Inventory	First Week Assembly	Second Week Assembly	Finished Goods Inventory
1	20–15*	5				24–24			
2	15–10	5	5			24–24			
3	10–5	5	5	5		24–24			
4	5–0	5	5	5	5–1	24–20	4		
5	60–55	5	5	5	6–2	20–16	4	4	0–4
6	55–50	5	5	5	7–3	16–12	4	4	0–8
7	50–45	5	5	5	8–4	60–56	4	4	8–12
8	45–40	5	5	5	9–5	56–52	4	4	12–16
9	40–35	5	5	5	10–6	52–48	4	4	16–20
10	35–30	5	5	5	11–7	48–44	4	4	20–24
11	30–25	5	5	5	12–8	44–40	4	4	24–28
12	25–20	5	5	5	13–9	40–36	4	4	28–32

*All inventories are beginning of week—end of week; that is, in the raw materials inventory, there are twenty units at the beginning of week one and fifteen at the end of week one.

1. Beginning raw materials inventory = 20 units.

2. Beginning purchased parts inventory = 24 units.

3. Beginning fabricated parts inventory = 0.

4. Fabrication production rate = 5 units per week.

5. Assembly production rate = 4 units per week.

6. Raw materials ordered at beginning of period = 60 units.

7. Purchased parts ordered at beginning of period = 48 units.

Changes in Production Rates

Changes in production rates from one period to another result in moderate administrative costs. In addition, increases in production rates take time to effect. Exhibit A4 shows the relationship between the size of the production increase and the time required to implement this increase. The previous period's weekly production rate is the number of units that entered a department in the final week. Decreases in production rate take place immediately.

For example, any increase greater than 20 percent but less than or equal to 25 percent will take four weeks to accomplish. During these four weeks, there will be a linear increase in production rate until the desired rate is reached.

There is only one exception to this rule. There is a one-week lag in starting production on a new product; thereafter if sufficient raw materials and workers are available, production is taken into the fabrication department at the scheduled rate. The assembly production rate will depend on the fabricated parts and purchased parts inventories.

Predicting Actual Production Rate

If the production rate increase is being provided by newly hired or transferred men, prediction of the actual production rate becomes more complex. There must be sufficient raw materials, fabricated parts, and purchased parts available. There must be enough plant and equipment for the number of men assigned. If these inventories and facilities are available, the production rate actually achieved in any one week will be limited either by the rate at which the desired increase in production can be implemented or by the inefficiency of the new men.

The following example illustrates how these two factors determine production rate. Assume that in this department the production rate achieved in the final week of the preceding period was 1800 units and the desired production rate is 2700 units per week. Since a 50 percent increase is desired, nine weeks will be required to achieve this increase; (Table 3) in other words, the maximum increase that can be implemented is 100 units more each week (900 units increase ÷ 9 weeks required for the increase). The worksheet in Exhibit A5 can be continued: In this example, note that production rate is limited in the first seven weeks by the time required to implement a 50 percent increase in production; in the last five weeks, the production rate is limited by the inefficiency of the new men. The desired rate of 2700 units per week will not be achieved in this period.

Using this worksheet will enable you to predict accurately the rate at which goods will enter a department each week in the decision period. It will also enable you to calculate the amount of production you will achieve; adding up the production for all twelve weeks will equal production volume on the quarterly report.

Exhibit A4

Increase of desired weekly production rate over previous period's final weekly production rate	≤	10%	15%	20%	25%	30%	35%	40%	45%	50%	55%	60%	More than 60%
Number of weeks required to implement the desired increase		1	2	3	4	5	6	7	8	9	10	11	12

Exhibit A5

Worksheet[1] (continued from Exhibit A2)

Week	1	2	3	4	5	6	7	8	9	10	11	12
8. Weekly production rate (add lines 2–7)	2231	2288	2344	2395	2448	2493	2528	2564	2591	2617	2635	2656
9. Amount of desired rate increase that can be implemented each week	100	200	300	400	500	600	700	800	900	900	900	900
10. Total possible production rate (line 9 + previous period's weekly rate)	1900	2000	2100	2200	2300	2400	2500	2600	2700	2700	2700	2700
11. Actual production rate per week (line 8 or 10, whichever is less)	1900	2000	2100	2200	2300	2400	2500	2564	2591	2617	2635	2656

[1] In this example, note that the production rate is limited

Appendix B

Terminal Based Planning Models for Use in Conjunction with the Management Simulation Sessions

To relieve you from certain time-consuming number-pushing activities four computer terminal based planning models have been developed. Effective use of those models will permit you to answer such simple (but time-consuming) questions as the following:

1. If a product generates a certain level of unit sales, what profit and return on investment figures will be created?

2. If a product generates a certain level of unit sales, what will the impact be on the firm's cash flow?

3. If a production rate increase is scheduled for a product, how much actual production will be generated in the period?

The remainder of this appendix describes in detail the output generated by each model and how to use it. To use any of the models, you must go to a terminal, and go through a sequence of activities described by your instructor to establish contact with the model.

Section I — 1 Quarter Profit

Purpose: This model will translate your forecast of product sales into pro forma estimates of profitability and assets required to support the product.

1. Sales units (000s)

2. Price

3. Cost/unit

4. Advertising (000s)

5. Product Development (000s)

The computer will then automatically provide you with estimates of the product income statement and net assets needed to support the product or a summary report consisting of net assets, operating profit, and operating profit/net assets ratio. (These estimates are accurate within ± $15,000.) A sample of the output provided you is shown in Exhibit B1 at the end of this section. An explanation of the procedures used to calculate each of the numbers on Exhibit B1 is also presented at the end of this section. This model should enable you to rapidly understand the specific financial consequences of a given sales forecast for one product for one period.

How to Use.

1. You type *run*; the terminal will respond with a message reading, *Type in your estimates for the values requested.* It will then type *Sales units* = and a question mark. You will then type in the forecasted sales (in 000s of units) and hit the return key.

2. The terminal will type *Price* = and a question mark. You will type in a unit price and hit the return key. In a like manner, you will insert figures for cost/unit, advertising budget (in 000s of dollars), and product development budget (in 000s of dollars).

3. The terminal will then type the message, *To obtain a full printout, type '1'. For a summary, type '2'.* (If you type a 1 you will receive a printout of the balance sheet and income statement. By typing a 2 you will obtain a summary consisting of net assets, operating profit, and the ratio of operating profit/net assets.) The terminal will then type a question mark and wait for you to type a 1 or a 2, depending upon which type of output you desire to have printed out. After you have typed a 1 or a 2, hit the return key.

4. The computer will then automatically prepare the balance sheet and profit and loss statement or the summary, depending on which you asked for.

5. After preparing the financial statements, the terminal will stop. To examine the profitability of another sales forecast or product description, simply type *run*, and hit the return key. You are now ready to repeat the entire procedure.

Explanation of Exhibit B1 for 1 Quarter Profit

The format of Exhibit B1 is the same as the income statement and the asset portion of the balance sheet produced in the management simulation. (The only figure omitted is one for overtime premium of the income statement.) Thus, although all figures on

Exhibit B1

Input and Output Format — 1QP

(A)

>RUN
TYPE IN YOUR ESTIMATES OF THE VALUES REQUESTED.
AFTER EACH ENTRY PRESS THE SPACE BAR'

SALES UNITS (000'S) = ? 300
PRICE = ? 8.30
COST/UNIT = ? 3.20
ADVERTISING (000'S) = ? 150
PROD DEVEL (000'S = ? 90

TO OBTAIN A FULL PRINTOUT, TYPE '1'. FOR A SUMMARY, TYPE '2'. ? 1

ALL VALUES ARE GIVEN IN THOUSANDS.

BALANCE SHEET			INCOME STATEMENT		
CASH	81.82918		SALES		2490
ACCTS REC	846.9387				
INVENTORIES			DIRECT MFG COSTS		
107.3684			305.5263		
59.21052			213.9473		
313.1907			322.1052		
52.30263			118.421		960
96	628.0723				1530
CURR ASSETS	1556.84		FACTORY OVERHEAD		
PLANT	1327.543		0		
			98.007		
TOTAL ASSETS	2884.384		69.18		
			33.18859		200.3756
ACCTS PAYABLE	197.0394		SELLING + ADMIN		
			150		
NET ASSETS	1687.344		0		
			169.5		
			38.85868		
			90		
			0		
			61.038	509.3966	
			OPERATING PROFIT	820.2277	
			OP PROFIT/NET ASSETS	.3052186	

(B)

>RUN
TYPE IN YOUR ESTIMATES OF THE VALUES REQUESTED.
AFTER EACH ENTRY PRESS THE SPACE BAR.

SALES UNITS (000's) = ? 300
PRICE = ? 8.30
COST/UNIT = ? 3.20
ADVERTISING (000'S) = ? 150
PROD DEVEL (000'S) = ? 90

TO OBTAIN A FULL PRINTOUT' TYPE '1'. FOR A SUMMARY, TYPE '2'. 2

NET ASSETS   2687.344
OPERATING PROFIT   820.2277
OPERATING PROFIT/
NET ASSETS   .3052186

Exhibit B1 are not alphabetically labeled, you can deduce their meaning by referring to the management simulation output reports. The key assumption used in preparing the balance sheet and income statement figures are listed as follows.

BALANCE SHEET

CASH = 5 percent of the cash expenditures that would be needed to support this product assuming 100 percent efficient factory, normal replacement of plant, and production level equal to sales level.

ACCTS REC = Approximately one third of the sales.

INVENTORIES = Raw materials calculated at raw material unit cost times one third of the sales rate; purchased parts calculated at purchased parts unit cost times one-half of sales rate; finished goods inventory calculated at 10 percent of unit sales times unit cost; fabricated parts calculated at one twelfth of sales rate times normal unit fabrication cost for a product of this total unit cost; inventory calculated using normal cost distribution between purchased parts, raw materials, fabrication, and assembly labor for a product of this total unit cost and a production rate equal to forecasted sales rate.*

PLANT = Calculated assuming $2312 of plant needed to support each worker. Number of workers calculated assuming production rate equal to forecasted sales and that all are 100 percent efficient.

ACCTS PAYABLE = Calculated as described on page 54.

INCOME STATEMENT

SALES = Unit price X forecasted unit sales.

DIRECT MFG COSTS = The total figure (1530 in Exhibit B1) calculated by multiplying sales units times cost/unit. The four component figures (305.5, etc. in Exhibit B1 are based on a normal breakdown between raw materials, fabrication labor, assembly labor, and purchased parts for a product of this cost/unit. As such, they will correspond *closely* but not *exactly* to your situation.

FACTORY OVERHEAD = Calculated according to data on page 48.

1. No idle men and all workers fully trained and 100 percent efficient.

2. Production level in each department is the same as sales volume.

3. Number of workers calculated by dividing $1.80 by the normal labor cost/unit for a product of this total cost/unit and multiplying the resulting figure by 500 and then dividing this new figure into the number of sales units forecasted.

*All unit costs referred to in this paragraph assume the normal breakdown between components parts of total unit cost as described on p. 9.

4. Plant value calculated by multiplying number of workers calculated in 3 above by $2300.

MARKETING AND ADMINISTRATION — Calculated according to data on pages 000. The following additional assumptions are made.

1. W.I.P. inventory calculated assuming level production for period.

2. Ending finished goods inventory assumed to be 10 percent of sales units.

3. Fabricated parts inventory assumed to be enough to support one week's production.

4. Raw materials unit inventory, one third of forecasted sales units.

5. Purchased parts unit inventory, one half of forecasted sales units.

Section II — 4 Quarter Profit

This model enables you to examine the financial impact of a specific set of production decisions and sales forecasts for a *particular product* for *four quarters* into the future. You provide the model with the following inputs.

1. Your sales forecasts and production schedules for each of the next four periods.

2. The price, cost/unit, marketing, and product development expenditures for each of the next four periods for the product.

3. The finished goods beginning inventory.

The computer will automatically provide you with estimates of the following items for each period.

1. Net assets required.

2. Operating profit.

3. Ratio of operating profit/net assets.

A sample of the input form and the output provided you is shown as Exhibit B2 (p.103). An explanation of the procedures used to calculate Exhibit B2's output is presented at the end of this section. This model should enable you to rapidly understand the financial consequences of your estimated sales forecasts and production schedules for a length of time up to four periods.

How to Use.

1. You type *run*; the terminal will respond with a message *Type in your estimates*

for the values requested. After each entry, press the space bar. The terminal will continue, typing a line which reads

Period: *1* *2* *3* *4.*

It will skip a line, type *sales units* and a question mark. You will type in your sales forecast (in 000s of units) for period 1, press the space bar (or type a coma if so instructed), type in your unit sales forecast for period 2, and so forth. (These figures should be expressed in thousands. For example, for a 200,000 unit forecast, you would type 200.)

2. When you have finished typing in your unit sales forecasts, hit the return key and the terminal will skip forward and type *prod units.* In a similar manner to the unit sales forecasts, type in your production estimates (in 000s of units) for each of the four periods. When you have typed in your estimate of unit production for period 4, hit the return key.

3. After sales and production units, you will key in price, cost/unit, advertising (in 000s), and product development (in 000s) for each of the four periods. After typing in the finished goods beginning inventory figure, hit the return key. The terminal will then type *index*, skip forward a line, and type a question mark. At this point you may change any line or lines by referring to Exhibit B3 (p.104). If you have made no mistakes, or once you have made all of the desired corrections, type a zero for the index. The computer will automatically provide figures for the four period's net asset requirements, operating profit, and ratio of operating profit to net assets.

4. Once the computer has provided the figures for net assets, operating profit, and ratio of operating profit to net assets, it will type out the following message: *You are now at the start of the model again. You may change any indexes you wish. index ?*

    Essentially what this means is that you are in a *run* position again. But instead of having to type *all* of the values in again, you need only refer to Exhibit B3 (p.104) to change any of the variables you wish, thus allowing yourself to examine another set of conditions. When you have completed your changes, you will still be asked for an index. Type a zero and the model will run forward.

Errors.

1. If you make an error typing in a value, do not worry. Keep going until you have keyed in all the values. When you have finished typing the last value and the terminal types *index*, simply follow the instructions described in step 3 of the foregoing section.

2. If you key in a figure containing an alphabetical character, the computer will become confused, throw you out of the program mode, and type a $>$ sign. At this point, your only alternative is to type *run* and begin again.

Procedures Used to Calculate Exhibit B2

This model's arithmetic is based on the same assumptions as the 1 quarter profit model with the following exceptions.

1. The terminal checks to see if your production and finished goods inventories are adequate to cover the sales forecasts. If they are not adequate, the sales forecast is reduced to a level that can be covered by the production and a message is printed out indicating that this has occurred.

2. Since the production and sales rates can be different, this feature is used in calculating the factory overhead and selling and administrative expenses.

3. An actual finished goods inventory figure is used.

Additionally, it should be noted that the model assumes 100 percent production efficiency even for cases where there are substantial increases in period to period manufacturing rates.

Section III — Production

Purpose. This model will provide you with an estimate of the amount of production you may expect from your factory under a given set of decisions. You will provide the model with the following statistics for the fabrication and assembly department.

1. Old production rate.

2. New production rate.

3. Labor cost/unit.

4. Number of workers in department who were previously employed there.

5. Number of newly hired workers in the department.

6. Number of workers newly transferred to the department.

7. Beginning efficiency of newly transferred workers.

8. Number of workers in department transferred from the idle labor pool.

9. Number of overtime hours scheduled.

You will also provide data on plant capacity and the size of raw materials, PURCHASED parts, and fabricated parts inventories.

The computer will automatically provide you with estimates of average worker efficiency and unit production during the quarter together with the ending value of fabricated

Exhibit B2

Exhibit B2

Input and Output Format — 4 QP

> RUN

TYPE IN YOUR ESTIMATES OF THE VALUES REQUESTED.
PRESS THE SPACE BAR AFTER EACH ENTRY.

PERIOD:		1		2		3		4
SALES UNITS (000'S)	?	350	?	450	?	500	?	607
PROD UNITS (000'S)		?	500	?	500	?	500	?	400
PRICE		?	5.0	?	5.0	?	5.0	?	5.0
COST/UNIT		?	1.8	?	1.8	?	1.8	?	1.8
ADVERTISING (000'S)		?	400	?	400	?	400	?	400
PROD DEVEL (000'S)		?	100	?	100	?	100	?	100
FIN GDS BEG INVEN (000'S) =		?	50						

INDEX
? 0

ALL VALUES GIVEN IN THOUSANDS.

	PERIOD 1	PERIOD 2	PERIOD 3	PERIOD 4
NET ASSETS (000'S)	2190.977	2536.588	2659.14	2355.97
OPERATING PRO (000'S)	179.8035	402.75555	514.4989	780.7845
OPERATING PRO/ NET ASSETS	.08	.16	.19	.33

YOUR ARE NOW AT THE START OF THE MODEL AGAIN. YOU MAY CHANGE ANY
INDEXES YOU WISH.

INDEX
?

Exhibit B3

CHANGING OF DATA IN 4Q MODEL

LINE TO BE CHANGED	INDEX
SALES UNITS[1]	1
PROD UNITS[1]	2
PRICE[1]	3
COST/UNIT[1]	4
ADVERTISING[1]	5
PROD DEVEL[1]	6
FIN GDS BEG INVEN	7

[1]Even though you may wish to alter one period's value, you must still retype the values for the other three periods.

parts inventory. A sample of the output provided you is shown as Exhibit B5 (p. 109). This model essentially follows the procedures outlined in Appendix A. However, it performs the calculation error-free in a fraction of the time it would take you to do them. This feature becomes increasingly important if you are not satisfied with the results of the first decision set and want to try another one.

How to Use.

1. Type *run*. The terminal will respond with a message reading *Type in your estimates of the values requested. After each entry, press the space bar.* It will then skip a line, print two headings reading *fabrication and assembly,* and after starting the succeeding line with the phrase, *old prod rates,* stop and print a question mark.

2. You should type in the previous period's ending fabrication department's production rate (in 000s of units), and hit the return key.*

3. Then type in the previous period's decision ending assembly department production rate (in 000s of units).

4. Similarly, key in figures for the NEW PROD RATES (in 000s of units) and LABOR COST/UNIT.*

5. Key in figures for OLD MEN (number of workers to work in the department, this period who worked there the previous period) HIRED MEN (new hires this period), and TRANSFERRED MEN (number of men transferred in from some other department).

6. Key in a figure for BEG EFF OF TRANSFERS for each department (between 0 and 1 representing the first week's efficiency of transferred workers). To calculate this figure, you will first have to decide from which department they are coming and then consult Appendix A to decide how efficient they will be.

7. Key in figures for *IDLE MEN* (the number of men transferred in from the idle labor pool to each department), and finally the number of overtime hours scheduled in each department.

8. The terminal will then ask you to key in (in 000s of units) RAW MATERIALS, PURCHASED PARTS and FABRICATED PARTS on hand at the beginning of the period. The final figure you will provide is the amount of plant (in 000s of dollars) available for *this product*. Your plant must be allocated between the products on the basis of the number of workers assigned to each product.

9. Exhibit B4 (p.107) demonstrates what your terminal output will look like at this point. Then as in the 4 quarter Profit model, the terminal will ask you for an index, print a question mark, and pause. If you have made a typing error or if you wish to change any of your values, refer to Exhibit B6 (p.110) for the appropriate index.

---

*Determined for fabrication by taking last quarter's ending fabrication W.I.P. inventory and multiplying by 4. Determined for assembly by taking last quarter's ending assembly W.I.P. inventory and multiplying by 6.

After typing the index corresponding to the line that you wish to change, hit the return key. The computer will print out the appropriate line so you can insert new values. For example, if you type a 1 for the index, the terminal will type out OLD PROD (in 000s of units), skip forward, print a question mark, and wait for you to key in an appropriate value for fabrication. After typing this value, hit the return key.

The terminal will move forward, print another question mark, and pause for you to insert a value for assembly.

After keying in the values required for that line, press the return key; the terminal will skip to a new line and again type INDEX and a question mark. You may then correct another line (or even the same one if you are particularly indecisive or low in manual dexterity). After you have finished correcting all the lines, you will still be asked for an INDEX. Type zero and the terminal will respond by providing you with the following output.

1. Worker efficiency for both fabrication and assembly.

2. Department output for both fabrication and assembly.

3. Standard labor CPU for both fabrication and assembly.

4. Actual labor CPU for both fabrication and assembly.

5. Ending W.I.P. inventory for both fabrication and assembly.

6. Fabricated parts inventory.

Also, the following additional information will automatically be provided for you:

1. 10 percent more beginning inventory.

2. 1000 hours more overtime.

3. 10 percent more plant.

4. 10 percent more men.

5. 10 percent higher production rate.

6. Total actual labor CPU for each of the foregoing figures.

Each of these figures is calculated to show the effect on production for both fabrication and assembly. The numbers are not cumulative. Rather, they are introduced to illustrate what effect (if there is, indeed, any effect at all) a 10 percent increase, or in the case of overtime, 1000 hours, in any *one* of these variables would have on your production rate for *both* fabrication and assembly. An example of the output can be found in Exhibit B5 (p. 109). After being provided with this output, you will then be asked for an INDEX. Again refer to Exhibit B6 to change any variables in order to examine a new set of conditions. When you have completed the changes, type zero for the INDEX, and the program will be initialized.

Exhibit B4

INPUT FORMAT FOR PROD

```
> RUN
TYPE IN YOUR ESTIMATES OF THE VALUES REQUESTED.
PRESS THE SPACE BAR AFTER EACH ENTRY.
```

	FAB.		ASSEM.
OLD PROD (∅∅∅'S)	? 36∅	?	36∅
NEW PROD (∅∅∅'S)	? 4∅∅	?	4∅∅
LABOR COST/UNIT	? 1.∅	?	0.7∅

DEPT WORK FORCE PROFILE:

	FAB.		ASSEM.
PREVIOUS EMPLOYEES	? 25∅	?	26∅
NEW HIRES	? 1∅	?	5
MEN TRANS FROM OTHER DEPTS	? 2	?	13
1ST WEEK EFF TRANS EMPLOYEES	? .95	?	.95
MEN FROM IDLE LABOR POOL	? ∅	?	∅
OVERTIME HOURS	? 1∅∅∅	?	11∅∅

INVENTORIES:

```
RAW MAT (∅∅∅'S) = ? 11∅
PUR PARTS (∅∅∅'S) = ? 7∅
FAB PARTS (∅∅∅'S) = ? 1∅∅

PLANT (∅∅∅'S) = ? 23∅∅

INDEX
? ∅
```

NEW FAB PROD HAS BEEN SCALED DOWN TO	238
NEW ASSEM PROD HAS BEEN SCALED DOWN TO	36∅

Errors.

1. If you make an error typing in a value, do not worry. Keep going until you have keyed in all the values. When you have finished typing the last value and the terminal types INDEX, simply follow the instructions described in step 9 of the previous section.

2. If you key in a figure containing an alphabetical character, the computer will become confused, throw you out of the program mode, and type a > sign. At this point, your only alternative is to type RUN and begin again.

Procedures Used to Calculate Exhibit B5

This model is almost an exact replica of the factory used in the Management Simulation. If you provide accurate values for each of the items in Exhibit B4, your actual production should differ from forecasted production by, at most, a few hundred units.

Section IV — N Quarter Cash Flow

Purpose. This model will provide you with an estimate of the cash flow you may expect this period and any subsequent period under a given set of decisions and estimated consequences. You will provide the model with the following data.

1. Your industry and firm number and the number of quarters forecasted.

2. *Product Statistics.* Sales Forecasts (in 000s of units); Production rate this quarter; Production rate next quarter.

3. *Plant Data.* Number of workers this quarter; plant ordered this quarter ($000s) overtime expenses ($000s).

4. *Other Data.* Advertising expenditure ($000s), product development, promotion and marketing research expenditure ($000s).

The computer will automatically provide you with estimates of net cash flow from operations, ending cash balance for the quarter, and the difference between this cash balance and the minimum figure required. At the same time, the computer will update all quantities so you will be ready for the next quarter. The format of this information is shown in Exhibit B7 (p. 113). Specific assumptions incorporated in the structure of this model are similar to those in 4 quarter profit. There is nothing provided by the model that you could not work out by yourself with paper and pencil, provided that you had enough time and were not prone to making errors. Its use should enable you to be far more sophisticated in your cash analysis than was possible previously.

Exhibit B5

OUTPUT FORMAT FOR PROD

	FABRICATION	ASSEMBLY
WORKER EFFICIENCY	98.4	69.4
DEPARTMENT OUTPUT	264378	249748
STANDARD LABOR CPU	1	.7
ACTUAL LABOR CPU	1.02	1.02
ENDING WIP INVENTORY	59238	60000

114630

	FAB OUTPUT	ASSEM OUTPUT	TOT ACT LABOR CPU
10 PERCENT MORE			
BEG INVEN	264378	256748	2.01
1000 HRS MORE OVTM	265728	250000	2.06
10 PERCENT MORE PLANT	264378	249748	2.04
10 PERCENT MORE MEN	268497	250000	2.21
10 PERCENT HIGHER			
PROD RATE	264378	249751	2.03

INDEX
?

Exhibit B6

CHANGING OF DATA IN PRODUCTION MODEL

LINE TO BE CHANGED	INDEX
OLD PROD (000s)	1
NEW PROD (000s)	2
LABOR COST/UNIT	3
PREVIOUS EMPLOYEES	4
NEW HIRES	5
TRANSFERRED MEN	6
BEG EFF TRANSFERS	7
IDLE MEN	8
OVERTIME HOURS	9
RAW MAT[1] (000s)	10
PUR PARTS[1] (000s)	10
FAB PARTS[1] (000s)	10
PLANT (000s)	11

[1] Please note that to change any *one* of these, you must key in values for *all three*.

How to Use.

1. Type *run* and hit the return key. The terminal will respond by asking you to indicate first your industry number and then your firm number.

2. You will then be asked to provide the following information for *each* of your products. (If you have only two products, simply type in zeros for Product 3.)

SALES FORECAST — These should be expressed in 000s of units.

PROD RATE THIS PERIOD — This is the rate at which you intend to produce in the coming period. This should be expressed in 000s.

PROD RATE NEXT PERIOD — This is the rate at which you intend to produce the following period. This should be expressed in 000s.

3. Next you will provide plant information covering all of your products.

NUMBER OF WORKERS EMPLOYED THIS PERIOD — Total number of workers (including idle men) you will have employed in this coming period.

OVERTIME THIS PERIOD — Total overtime for all products for coming period expressed in 000s dollars.

PLANT ORDERED THIS PERIOD — Total plant in 000s of dollars you will *order* in the coming period.

4. Then you will be asked to provide total ADVERTISING and PROD DEV, prom, and MKT RES both in 000s of dollars for your products.

5. Finally you will indicate over how many quarters you wish to forecast your cash flow.

6. The model will then automatically read from a date file the information pertinent to your particular firm.

> Beginning cash balance ($000s)
> Accounts receivable ($000s)
> Accounts payable ($000s)
> No. of workers employed last period
> Total present plant ($000s)
> Plant ordered last period ($000s)

and for each of the following products.

> Unit price
> Raw materials cost
> Purchased parts cost
> Finished goods inventory (000s units)
> Raw materials inventory (000s units)
> Purchased parts inventory (000s units)

7. If you are doing a cash flow for more than one period, you must be sure to use index 19 to insert a value for taxes payable for the second or any succeeding quarters. This value will be added to the calculated beginning cash balance to provide you with a more accurate cash flow.

8. After you have filled in the last entry, hit the return key. The terminal will then type *index* and a question mark. At this point you have two options.

   a. If you have made no typing errors and are ready to run, type a zero for the index and hit the return key. You will automatically be provided with a cash flow statement for the first quarter.

   b. If you have made a typing error or wish to make a change in any item, refer to Exhibit B8 (p. 114) for the appropriate index to correct it. When you have finished making the corrections, you will still be asked for an index, type a zero. The terminal will respond with the cash flow statement.

9. After the forecast has been printed out, the terminal will again ask for an index. If you want to change any of the foregoing steps to prepare the following quarter's statement, merely repeat the procedures outlined in step 8 above.

Assumptions

To reconcile the output of this model with the actual cash flow statement you should note the following.

1. The sales forecasts must be the same as the actual sales.

2. This model does not include any cash flows relating to

   a. Dividend payments.

   b. Interest payments or tax thereon.

   c. Loan principal repayments.

   d. Sale of stock.

   e. Purchase or sale of securities or security income.

   f. Tax payments after the first period you are examining.

3. This model assumes no indirect labor expenditures (i.e., 100 percent efficient workers).

Subject to these constraints the output of this model should provide results within $75,000 of the actual figures.

Exhibit B7

INPUT AND OUTPUT FORMAT FOR NCSH

```
> RUN
TYPE IN YOUR INDUSTRY NUMBER      ?    41
TYPE IN YOUR FIRM NUMBER            ?   1
```

PRODUCT:

PRODUCT:	1	2	3
SALES FORECASTS	? 46?	44∅ ?	∅
PROD RATE THIS PERIOD (∅∅∅'S)	? 16.25?	6.75 ?	∅

PLANT:

```
NO. OF WORKERS EMPLOYED THIS PERIOD = ? 895
OVERTIME THIS PERIOD    ($∅∅∅'S) = ? 352
PLANT ORDERED THIS PERIOD (∅∅∅'S) = ? ∅
```

OTHER DECISION DATA ($∅∅∅'S):

```
ADVERTISING = 79∅
PROD DEV, PROM, & MKT RES = ? 1
```

```
INDEX
? ∅
```

UNIT SALES HAVE BEEN SCALED DOWN TO 13∅.48 FOR PRODUCT 2

ALL VALUES ARE GIVEN IN THOUSANDS

1   QUARTER CASH FLOW FORECAST

QUARTER	BEG. CASH BALANCE	NET CASH FLOW FROM OPERATIONS	ENDING CASH BALANCE	ENDING CASH BAL. MINUS MIN. REG. CASH BAL.
1	134.∅8	−471.241	−337.161	−497.295

```
>
```

Exhibit B8

ERROR CORRECTION FOR N QUARTER CASH FLOW

ITEM TO BE CHANGED	INDEX
BEG CASH BAL ($000s)[1]	1
ACCTS REC ($000s)[1]	1
ACCTS PAY ($000s)[1]	1
SALES FORECASTS (000s OF UNITS)[2]	2
UNIT PRICE[2]	3
RAW MAT COST[2]	4
PUR PARTS COST[2]	5
PROD RATE THIS PERIOD (000s)[2]	6
PROD RATE NEXT PERIOD (000s)[2]	7
FIN GDS INVEN (000s OF UNITS)[2]	8
RAW MAT INVEN (000s OF UNITS)[2]	9
PUR PARTS INVEN (000s OF UNITS)[2]	10
NO. OF WORKERS EMPLOYED LAST PERIOD[2]	11
NO. OF WORKERS EMPLOYED THIS PERIOD[2]	12
OVERTIME THIS PERIOD ($000s)[2]	13
TOTAL PRESENT PLANT ($000s)[2]	14
PLANT ORDERED LAST PERIOD ($000s)[2]	15
PLANT ORDERED THIS PERIOD ($000s)[2]	16
ADVERTISING ($000s)[3]	17
PROD DEV, PROM, AND MARKET RES ($000s)[3]	17
NUMBER OF QUARTERS FORECASTED	18
TAXES PAYABLE	19

[1] To change any *one* of these you must retype values for *all* three.

[2] Although you may wish to change a value for only one product, you must retype the values for the other two.

[3] To change one of these, you must retype the value for the other variable.

Decision
Forms

Industry _____ Firm _____ Period _____ Section _____

Purchase Plant $1000	Purchase Securities $1000	Dividends $1000	90-Day Loans $1000	One-Year Loan $1000	Five-Year Notes $1000	Sell Stock $1000	
							1

PRODUCT 1

Price Next Period $ per unit	Advertising Budget $1000	Promotion Budget $1000	Prod. Dev. Budget $1000	Mkt. Res. Budget $1000	MR– Price ¢ PU	MR– Adv. $1000	MR– Qual. ¢ PU	MR– P.D. $1000	
									2

Raw Mat'l $ per unit	Fab. Production Rate Next Pd. (Anticipated) 1000 units	Fab. Labor $ per unit	Fab. # Men Assigned	# Men Hired Or Fired (–)	Fab. Overtime # Hours	
						3

Purchased Parts $ per unit	Asm. Production Rate Next Pd. (Anticipated) 1000 unites	Asm. Labor $ per unit	Asm. # Men Assigned	# Men Hired Or Fired (–)	Asm. Overtime # Hours	
						4

PRODUCT 2

Price Next Period $ per unit	Advertising Budget $1000	Promotion Budget $1000	Prod. Dev. Budget $1000	Mkt. Res. Budget $1000	MR– Price ¢ PU	MR– Adv. $1000	MR– Qual. ¢ PU	MR– P.D. $1000	
									5

Raw Mat'l $ per unit	Fab. Production Rate Next Pd. (Anticipated) 1000 units	Fab. Labor $ per unit	Fab. # Men Assigned	# Men Hired Or Fired (–)	Fab. Overtime # Hours	
						6

Purchased Parts $ per units	Asm. Production Rate Next Pd. (Anticipated) 1000 units	Asm. Labor $ per unit	Asm. # Men Assigned	# Men Hired Or Fired (–)	Asm. Overtime # Hours	
						7

Product 3

Price Next Period $ per unit	Advertising Budget $1000	Promotion Budget $1000	Prod. Dev. Budget $1000	Mkt. Res. Budget $1000	MR– Price ¢ PU	MR– Adv. $1000	MR– Qual. ¢ PU	MR– P.D. $1000	
									8

Raw Mat'l $ per unit	Fab. Production Rate Next Pd. (Anticipated) 1000 units	Fab. Labor $ per unit	Fab. # Men Assigned	# Men Hired Or Fired (–)	Fab. Overtime # Hours	
						9

Purchased Parts $ per unit	Asm. Production Rate Next Pd. (Anticipated) 1000 units	Asm. Labor $ per unit	Asm. # Men Assigned	# Men Hired Or Fired (–)	Asm. Overtime # Hours	
						10

Industry _____ Firm _____ Period _____ Section _____

Purchase Plant $1000	Purchase Securities $1000	Dividends $1000	90-Day Loans $1000	One-Year Loan $1000	Five-Year Notes $1000	Sell Stock $1000			
									1

PRODUCT 1

Price Next Period $ per unit	Advertising Budget $1000	Promotion Budget $1000	Prod. Dev. Budget $1000	Mkt. Res. Budget $1000	MR— Price ¢ PU	MR— Adv. $1000	MR— Qual. ¢ PU	MR— P.D. $1000	
									2

Raw Mat'l $ per unit	Fab. Production Rate Next Pd. (Anticipated) 1000 units		Fab. Labor $ per unit	Fab. # Men Assigned	# Men Hired Or Fired (−)	Fab. Overtime # Hours	
							3

Purchased Parts $ per unit	Asm. Production Rate Next Pd. (Anticipated) 1000 unites		Asm. Labor $ per unit	Asm. # Men Assigned	# Men Hired Or Fired (−)	Asm. Overtime # Hours	
							4

PRODUCT 2

Price Next Period $ per unit	Advertising Budget $1000	Promotion Budget $1000	Prod. Dev. Budget $1000	Mkt. Res. Budget $1000	MR— Price ¢ PU	MR— Adv. $1000	MR— Qual. ¢ PU	MR— P.D. $1000	
									5

Raw Mat'l $ per unit	Fab. Production Rate Next Pd. (Anticipated) 1000 units		Fab. Labor $ per unit	Fab. # Men Assigned	# Men Hired Or Fired (−)	Fab. Overtime # Hours	
							6

Purchased Parts $ per units	Asm. Production Rate Next Pd. (Anticipated) 1000 units		Asm. Labor $ per unit	Asm. # Men Assigned	# Men Hired Or Fired (−)	Asm. Overtime # Hours	
							7

Product 3

Price Next Period $ per unit	Advertising Budget $1000	Promotion Budget $1000	Prod. Dev. Budget $1000	Mkt. Res. Budget $1000	MR— Price ¢ PU	MR— Adv. $1000	MR— Qual. ¢ PU	MR— P.D. $1000	
									8

Raw Mat'l $ per unit	Fab. Production Rate Next Pd. (Anticipated) 1000 units		Fab. Labor $ per unit	Fab. # Men Assigned	# Men Hired Or Fired (−)	Fab. Overtime # Hours	
							9

Purchased Parts $ per unit	Asm. Production Rate Next Pd. (Anticipated) 1000 units		Asm. Labor $ per unit	Asm. # Men Assigned	# Men Hired Or Fired (−)	Asm. Overtime # Hours	
							10

119

Industry _____ Firm _____ Period _____ Section _____

Purchase Plant $1000	Purchase Securities $1000	Dividends $1000	90-Day Loans $1000	One-Year Loan $1000	Five-Year Notes $1000	Sell Stock $1000	
							1

PRODUCT 1

Price Next Period $ per unit	Advertising Budget $1000	Promotion Budget $1000	Prod. Dev. Budget $1000	Mkt. Res. Budget $1000	MR— Price ¢ PU	MR— Adv. $1000	MR— Qual. ¢ PU	MR— P.D. $1000	
									2

Raw Mat'l $ per unit	Fab. Production Rate Next Pd. (Anticipated) 1000 units	Fab. Labor $ per unit	Fab. # Men Assigned	# Men Hired Or Fired (−)	Fab. Overtime # Hours	
						3

Purchased Parts $ per unit	Asm. Production Rate Next Pd. (Anticipated) 1000 unites	Asm. Labor $ per unit	Asm. # Men Assigned	# Men Hired Or Fired (−)	Asm. Overtime # Hours	
						4

PRODUCT 2

Price Next Period $ per unit	Advertising Budget $1000	Promotion Budget $1000	Prod. Dev. Budget $1000	Mkt. Res. Budget $1000	MR— Price ¢ PU	MR— Adv. $1000	MR— Qual. ¢ PU	MR— P.D. $1000	
									5

Raw Mat'l $ per unit	Fab. Production Rate Next Pd. (Anticipated) 1000 units	Fab. Labor $ per unit	Fab. # Men Assigned	# Men Hired Or Fired (−)	Fab. Overtime # Hours	
						6

Purchased Parts $ per units	Asm. Production Rate Next Pd. (Anticipated) 1000 units	Asm. Labor $ per unit	Asm. # Men Assigned	# Men Hired Or Fired (−)	Asm. Overtime # Hours	
						7

Product 3

Price Next Period $ per unit	Advertising Budget $1000	Promotion Budget $1000	Prod. Dev. Budget $1000	Mkt. Res. Budget $1000	MR— Price ¢ PU	MR— Adv. $1000	MR— Qual. ¢ PU	MR— P.D. $1000	
									8

Raw Mat'l $ per unit	Fab. Production Rate Next Pd. (Anticipated) 1000 units	Fab. Labor $ per unit	Fab. # Men Assigned	# Men Hired Or Fired (−)	Fab. Overtime # Hours	
						9

Purchased Parts $ per unit	Asm. Production Rate Next Pd. (Anticipated) 1000 units	Asm. Labor $ per unit	Asm. # Men Assigned	# Men Hired Or Fired (−)	Asm. Overtime # Hours	
						10

Industry _____ Firm _____ Period _____ Section _____

Purchase Plant $1000	Purchase Securities $1000	Dividends $1000	90-Day Loans $1000	One-Year Loan $1000	Five-Year Notes $1000	Sell Stock $1000	
							1

PRODUCT 1							
Price Next Period $ per unit	Advertising Budget $1000	Promotion Budget $1000	Prod. Dev. Budget $1000	Mkt. Res. Budget $1000	MR— Price ¢ PU	MR— Adv. $1000	MR— Qual. ¢ PU	MR— P.D. $1000
								2

Raw Mat'l $ per unit	Fab. Production Rate Next Pd. (Anticipated) 1000 units	Fab. Labor $ per unit	Fab. # Men Assigned	# Men Hired Or Fired (—)	Fab. Overtime # Hours	
						3

Purchased Parts $ per unit	Asm. Production Rate Next Pd. (Anticipated) 1000 unites	Asm. Labor $ per unit	Asm. # Men Assigned	# Men Hired Or Fired (—)	Asm. Overtime # Hours	
						4

PRODUCT 2							
Price Next Period $ per unit	Advertising Budget $1000	Promotion Budget $1000	Prod. Dev. Budget $1000	Mkt. Res. Budget $1000	MR— Price ¢ PU	MR— Adv. $1000	MR— Qual. ¢ PU	MR— P.D. $1000
								5

Raw Mat'l $ per unit	Fab. Production Rate Next Pd. (Anticipated) 1000 units	Fab. Labor $ per unit	Fab. # Men Assigned	# Men Hired Or Fired (—)	Fab. Overtime # Hours	
						6

Purchased Parts $ per units	Asm. Production Rate Next Pd. (Anticipated) 1000 units	Asm. Labor $ per unit	Asm. # Men Assigned	# Men Hired Or Fired (—)	Asm. Overtime # Hours	
						7

Product 3							
Price Next Period $ per unit	Advertising Budget $1000	Promotion Budget $1000	Prod. Dev. Budget $1000	Mkt. Res. Budget $1000	MR— Price ¢ PU	MR— Adv. $1000	MR— Qual. ¢ PU	MR— P.D. $1000
								8

Raw Mat'l $ per unit	Fab. Production Rate Next Pd. (Anticipated) 1000 units	Fab. Labor $ per unit	Fab. # Men Assigned	# Men Hired Or Fired (—)	Fab. Overtime # Hours	
						9

Purchased Parts $ per unit	Asm. Production Rate Next Pd. (Anticipated) 1000 units	Asm. Labor $ per unit	Asm. # Men Assigned	# Men Hired Or Fired (—)	Asm. Overtime # Hours	
						10

123

Industry _____ Corporation _____ Division _____ Period _____ Section _____

PRODUCT 1

Price Next Period $ per unit	Advertising Budget $1000	Promotion Budget $1000	Prod. Dev. Budget $1000	Mkt. Res. Budget $1000	MR— Price ¢ PU	MR— Adv. $1000	MR— Qual. ¢ PU	MR— P.D. $1000	
									2

Raw Mat'l $ per unit	Fab. Production Rates Next Pd. 1000 units	This Pd. 1000 units	Fab. Labor $ per unit	Fab. # Men Assigned	# Men Hired Or Fired (—)	Fab. Overtime # Hours	
							3

Purchased Parts $ per unit	Asm Production Rates Next Pd. 1000 units	This Pd. 1000 units	Asm. Labor $ per unit	Asm. # Men Assigned	# Men Hired Or Fired (—)	Asm. Overtime # Hours	
							4

PRODUCT 2

Price Next Period $ per unit	Advertising Budget $1000	Promotion Budget $1000	Prod. Dev. Budget $1000	Mkt. Res. Budget $1000	MR— Price ¢ PU	MR— Adv. $1000	MR— Qual. ¢ PU	MR— P.D. $1000	
									5

Raw Mat'l $ per unit	Fab. Production Rates Next Pd. 1000 units	This Pd. 1000 units	Fab. Labor $ per unit	Fab. # Men Assigned	# Men Hired Or Fired (—)	Fab. Overtime # Hours	
							6

Purchased Parts $ per units	Asm. Production Rates Next Pd. 1000 units	This pd. 1000 units	Asm. Labor $ per unit	Asm. # Men Assigned	# Men Hired Or Fired (—)	Asm. Overtime # Hours	
							7

PRODUCT 3

Price Next Period $ per unit	Advertising Budget $1000	Promotion Budget $1000	Prod. Dev. Budget $1000	Mkt. Res. Budget $1000	MR— Price ¢ PU	MR— Adv. $1000	MR— Qual. ¢ PU	MR— P.D. $1000	
									8

Raw Mat'l $ per unit	Fab. Production Rates Next Pd. 1000 units	This Pd. 1000 units	Fab. Labor $ per unit	Fab. # Men Assigned	# Men Hired Or Fired (—)	Fab. Overtime # Hours	
							9

Purchased Parts $ per unit	Asm. Production Rates Next Pd. 1000 units	This Pd. 1000 units	Asm. Labor $ per unit	Asm. # Men Assigned	# Men Hired Or Fired (—)	Asm. Overtime # Hours	
							10

Industry _____ Corporation _____ Division _____ Period _____ Section _____

PRODUCT 1								
Price Next Period $ per unit	Advertising Budget $1000	Promotion Budget $1000	Prod. Dev. Budget $1000	Mkt. Res. Budget $1000	MR– Price ¢ PU	MR– Adv. $1000	MR– Qual. ¢ PU	MR– P.D. $1000
								2

	Fab. Production Rates							
Raw Mat'l $ per unit	Next Pd. 1000 units	This Pd. 1000 units	Fab. Labor $ per unit	Fab. # Men Assigned	# Men Hired Or Fired (–)		Fab. Overtime # Hours	
								3

	Asm Production Rates							
Purchased Parts $ per unit	Next Pd. 1000 units	This Pd. 1000 units	Asm. Labor $ per unit	Asm. # Men Assigned	# Men Hired Or Fired (–)		Asm. Overtime # Hours	
								4

PRODUCT 2								
Price Next Period $ per unit	Advertising Budget $1000	Promotion Budget $1000	Prod. Dev. Budget $1000	Mkt. Res. Budget $1000	MR– Price ¢ PU	MR– Adv. $1000	MR– Qual. ¢ PU	MR– P.D. $1000
								5

	Fab. Production Rates							
Raw Mat'l $ per unit	Next Pd. 1000 units	This Pd. 1000 units	Fab. Labor $ per unit	Fab. # Men Assigned	# Men Hired Or Fired (–)		Fab. Overtime # Hours	
								6

	Asm. Production Rates							
Purchased Parts $ per units	Next Pd. 1000 units	This pd. 1000 units	Asm. Labor $ per unit	Asm. # Men Assigned	# Men Hired Or Fired (–)		Asm. Overtime # Hours	
								7

PRODUCT 3								
Price Next -Period $ per unit	Advertising Budget $1000	Promotion Budget $1000	Prod. Dev. Budget $1000	Mkt. Res. Budget $1000	MR– Price ¢ PU	MR– Adv. $1000	MR– Qual. ¢ PU	MR– P.D. $1000
								8

	Fab. Production Rates							
Raw Mat'l $ per unit	Next Pd. 1000 units	This Pd. 1000 units	Fab. Labor $ per unit	Fab. # Men Assigned	# Men Hired Or Fired (–)		Fab. Overtime # Hours	
								9

	Asm. Production Rates							
Purchased Parts $ per unit	Next Pd. 1000 units	This Pd. 1000 units	Asm. Labor $ per unit	Asm. # Men Assigned	# Men Hired Or Fired (–)		Asm. Overtime # Hours	
								10

127

MANAGEMENT SIMULATION – DIVISION DECISION FORM

Industry _____ Corporation _____ Division _____ Period _____ Section _____

PRODUCT 1

Price Next Period $ per unit	Advertising Budget $1000	Promotion Budget $1000	Prod. Dev. Budget $1000	Mkt. Res. Budget $1000	MR– Price ¢ PU	MR– Adv. $1000	MR– Qual. ¢ PU	MR– P.D. $1000	
									2

Raw Mat'l $ per unit	Fab. Production Rates Next Pd. 1000 units	This Pd. 1000 units	Fab. Labor $ per unit	Fab. # Men Assigned	# Men Hired Or Fired (–)	Fab. Overtime # Hours	
							3

Purchased Parts $ per unit	Asm Production Rates Next Pd. 1000 units	This Pd. 1000 units	Asm. Labor $ per unit	Asm. # Men Assigned	# Men Hired Or Fired (–)	Asm. Overtime # Hours	
							4

PRODUCT 2

Price Next Period $ per unit	Advertising Budget $1000	Promotion Budget $1000	Prod. Dev. Budget $1000	Mkt. Res. Budget $1000	MR– Price ¢ PU	MR– Adv. $1000	MR– Qual. ¢ PU	MR– P.D. $1000	
									5

Raw Mat'l $ per unit	Fab. Production Rates Next Pd. 1000 units	This Pd. 1000 units	Fab. Labor $ per unit	Fab. # Men Assigned	# Men Hired Or Fired (–)	Fab. Overtime # Hours	
							6

Purchased Parts $ per units	Asm. Production Rates Next Pd. 1000 units	This pd. 1000 units	Asm. Labor $ per unit	Asm. # Men Assigned	# Men Hired Or Fired (–)	Asm. Overtime # Hours	
							7

PRODUCT 3

Price Next Period $ per unit	Advertising Budget $1000	Promotion Budget $1000	Prod. Dev. Budget $1000	Mkt. Res. Budget $1000	MR– Price ¢ PU	MR– Adv. $1000	MR– Qual. ¢ PU	MR– P.D. $1000	
									8

Raw Mat'l $ per unit	Fab. Production Rates Next Pd. 1000 units	This Pd. 1000 units	Fab. Labor $ per unit	Fab. # Men Assigned	# Men Hired Or Fired (–)	Fab. Overtime # Hours	
							9

Purchased Parts $ per unit	Asm. Production Rates Next Pd. 1000 units	This Pd. 1000 units	Asm. Labor $ per unit	Asm. # Men Assigned	# Men Hired Or Fired (–)	Asm. Overtime # Hours	
							10

Industry _____ Corporation _____ Division _____ Period _____ Section _____

PRODUCT 1									
Price Next Period $ per unit	Advertising Budget $1000	Promotion Budget $1000	Prod. Dev. Budget $1000	Mkt. Res. Budget $1000	MR– Price ¢ PU	MR– Adv. $1000	MR– Qual. ¢ PU	MR– P.D. $1000	
									2
Raw Mat'l $ per unit	Fab. Production Rates Next Pd. 1000 units	This Pd. 1000 units	Fab. Labor $ per unit	Fab. # Men Assigned	# Men Hired Or Fired (–)		Fab. Overtime # Hours		
									3
Purchased Parts $ per unit	Asm Production Rates Next Pd. 1000 units	This Pd. 1000 units	Asm. Labor $ per unit	Asm. # Men Assigned	# Men Hired Or Fired (–)		Asm. Overtime # Hours		
									4

PRODUCT 2									
Price Next Period $ per unit	Advertising Budget $1000	Promotion Budget $1000	Prod. Dev. Budget $1000	Mkt. Res. Budget $1000	MR– Price ¢ PU	MR– Adv. $1000	MR– Qual. ¢ PU	MR– P.D. $1000	
									5
Raw Mat'l $ per unit	Fab. Production Rates Next Pd. 1000 units	This Pd. 1000 units	Fab. Labor $ per unit	Fab. # Men Assigned	# Men Hired Or Fired (–)		Fab. Overtime # Hours		
									6
Purchased Parts $ per units	Asm. Production Rates Next Pd. 1000 units	This pd. 1000 units	Asm. Labor $ per unit	Asm. # Men Assigned	# Men Hired Or Fired (–)		Asm. Overtime # Hours		
									7

PRODUCT 3									
Price Next Period $ per unit	Advertising Budget $1000	Promotion Budget $1000	Prod. Dev. Budget $1000	Mkt. Res. Budget $1000	MR– Price ¢ PU	MR– Adv. $1000	MR– Qual. ¢ PU	MR– P.D. $1000	
									8
Raw Mat'l $ per unit	Fab. Production Rates Next Pd. 1000 units	This Pd. 1000 units	Fab. Labor $ per unit	Fab. # Men Assigned	# Men Hired Or Fired (–)		Fab. Overtime # Hours		
									9
Purchased Parts $ per unit	Asm. Production Rates Next Pd. 1000 units	This Pd. 1000 units	Asm. Labor $ per unit	Asm. # Men Assigned	# Men Hired Or Fired (–)		Asm. Overtime # Hours		
									10

MANAGEMENT SIMULATION – CORPORATE DECISION FORM

Corporation _____ Period _____ Section _____

External Financial Decisions					
Purchase Securities ($1000	Dividends ($1000)	90-Day Loans ($1000)	One Year Loans ($1000)	Five Year Notes ($1000)	Sell Stock ($1000)
/////	/////	/////	/////	/////	/////

Forecasted Earnings Per Share				
This Period	Next Period	Two Periods in Future	Three Periods in Future	/////
				/////
/////	/////	/////	/////	/////

Building and Equipment Purchases		
Division 1 ($1,000)	Division 2 ($1,000)	Division 3 ($1,000)
/////	/////	/////

Cash Transfers to and from Divisions		
Division 1	Division 2	Division 3
		/////

133

MANAGEMENT SIMULATION — CORPORATE DECISION FORM

Corporation _____ Period _____ Section _____

External Financial Decisions					
Purchase Securities ($1000	Dividends ($1000)	90-Day Loans ($1000)	One Year Loans ($1000)	Five Year Notes ($1000)	Sell Stock ($1000)
/////////	/////////	/////////	/////////	/////////	/////////

Forecasted Earnings Per Share				
This Period	Next Period	Two Periods in Future	Three Periods in Future	/////////
/////////	/////////	/////////	/////////	/////////

Building and Equipment Purchases		
Division 1 ($1,000)	Division 2 ($1,000)	Division 3 ($1,000)
/////////	/////////	/////////

Cash Transfers to and from Divisions			
Division 1	Division 2	Division 3	/////////
			/////////

MANAGEMENT SIMULATION — CORPORATE DECISION FORM

Corporation _____ Period _____ Section _____

External Financial Decisions					
Purchase Securities ($1000	Dividends ($1000)	90-Day Loans ($1000)	One Year Loans ($1000)	Five Year Notes ($1000)	Sell Stock ($1000)
/////////	/////////	/////////	/////////	/////////	/////////

Forecasted Earnings Per Share				
This Period	Next Period	Two Periods in Future	Three Periods in Future	/////////
/////////	/////////	/////////	/////////	/////////

Building and Equipment Purchases					
Division 1 ($1,000)		Division 2 ($1,000)		Division 3 ($1,000)	
/////////	/////////	/////////	/////////	/////////	/////////

Cash Transfers to and from Divisions			
Division 1	Division 2	Division 3	/////////

MANAGEMENT SIMULATION — CORPORATE DECISION FORM

Corporation _____ Period _____ Section _____

External Financial Decisions					
Purchase Securities ($1000	Dividends ($1000)	90-Day Loans ($1000)	One Year Loans ($1000)	Five Year Notes ($1000)	Sell Stock ($1000)

Forecasted Earnings Per Share				
This Period	Next Period	Two Periods in Future	Three Periods in Future	

Building and Equipment Purchases					
Division 1 ($1,000)		Division 2 ($1,000)		Division 3 ($1,000)	

Cash Transfers to and from Divisions			
Division 1	Division 2	Division 3	

Industry _____ Corporation _____ Div. –Plt. _____ Period _____ Section _____

PRODUCT 1								
Price Next Period $ per unit	Advertising Budget $1000	Promotion Budget $1000	Prod. Dev. Budget $1000	Mkt. Res. Budget $1000	MR– Price ¢ PU	MR– Adv. $1000	MR– Qual. ¢ PU	MR– P.D. $1000
								2

Raw Mat'l $ per unit	Fab. Production Rates		Fab. Labor $ per unit	Fab. # Men Assigned	# Men Hired Or Fired (–)	Fab. Overtime # Hours	
	Next Pd. 1000 units	This Pd. 1000 units					
							3

Purchased Parts $ per unit	Asm. Production Rates		Asm. Labor $ per unit	Asm. # Men Assigned	# Men Hired Or Fired (–)	Asm. Overtime # Hours	
	Next Pd. 1000 units	This Pd. 1000 units					
							4

PRODUCT 2								
Price Next Period $ per unit	Advertising Budget $1000	Promotion Budget $1000	Prod. Dev. Budget $1000	Mkt. Res. Budget $1000	MR– Price ¢ PU	MR– Adv. $1000	MR– Qual. ¢ PU	MR– P.D. $1000
								5

Raw Mat'l $ per unit	Fab. Production Rates		Fab. Labor $ per unit	Fab. # Men Assigned	# Men Hired Or Fired (–)	Fab. Overtime # Hours	
	Next Pd. 1000 units	This Pd. 1000 units					
							6

Purchased Parts $ per units	Asm. Production Rates		Asm. Labor $ per unit	Asm. # Men Assigned	# Men Hired Or Fired (–)	Asm. Overtime # Hours	
	Next Pd. 1000 units	This Pd. 1000 units					
							7

PRODUCT 3								
Price Next Period $ per unit	Advertising Budget $1000	Promotion Budget $1000	Prod. Dev. Budget $1000	Mkt. Res. Budget $1000	MR– Price ¢ PU	MR– Adv. $1000	MR– Qual. ¢ PU	MR– P.D. $1000
								8

Raw Mat'l $ per unit	Fab. Production Rates		Fab. Labor $ per unit	Fab # Men Assigned	# Men Hired Or Fired (–)	Fab. Overtime # Hours	
	Next Pd. 1000 units	This Pd. 1000 units					
							9

Purchased Parts $ per unit	Asm. Production Rates		Asm. Labor $ per unit	Asm. # Men Assigned	# Men Hired Or Fired (–)	Asm. Overtime # Hours	
	Next Pd. 1000 units	This Pd. 1000 units					
							10

Industry _____ Corporation _____ Div. –Plt._____ Period _____ Section _____

PRODUCT 1									
Price Next Period $ per unit	Advertising Budget $1000	Promotion Budget $1000	Prod. Dev. Budget $1000	Mkt. Res. Budget $1000	MR– Price ¢ PU	MR– Adv. $1000	MR– Qual. ¢ PU	MR– P.D. $1000	
									2
Raw Mat'l $ per unit	Fab. Production Rates Next Pd. 1000 units	This Pd. 1000 units	Fab. Labor $ per unit	Fab. # Men Assigned	# Men Hired Or Fired (–)		Fab. Overtime # Hours		
									3
Purchased Parts $ per unit	Asm. Production Rates Next Pd. 1000 units	This Pd. 1000 units	Asm. Labor $ per unit	Asm. # Men Assigned	# Men Hired Or Fired (–)		Asm. Overtime # Hours		
									4

PRODUCT 2									
Price Next Period $ per unit	Advertising Budget $1000	Promotion Budget $1000	Prod. Dev. Budget $1000	Mkt. Res. Budget $1000	MR– Price ¢ PU	MR– Adv. $1000	MR– Qual. ¢ PU	MR– P.D. $1000	
									5
Raw Mat'l $ per unit	Fab. Production Rates Next Pd. 1000 units	This Pd. 1000 units	Fab. Labor $ per unit	Fab. # Men Assigned	# Men Hired Or Fired (–)		Fab. Overtime # Hours		
									6
Purchased Parts $ per units	Asm. Production Rates Next Pd. 1000 units	This Pd. 1000 units	Asm. Labor $ per unit	Asm. # Men Assigned	# Men Hired Or Fired (–)		Asm. Overtime # Hours		
									7

PRODUCT 3									
Price Next Period $ per unit	Advertising Budget $1000	Promotion Budget $1000	Prod. Dev. Budget $1000	Mkt. Res. Budget $1000	MR– Price ¢ PU	MR– Adv. $1000	MR– Qual. ¢ PU	MR– P.D. $1000	
									8
Raw Mat'l $ per unit	Fab. Production Rates Next Pd. 1000 units	This Pd. 1000 units	Fab. Labor $ per unit	Fab # Men Assigned	# Men Hired Or Fired (–)		Fab. Overtime # Hours		
									9
Purchased Parts $ per unit	Asm. Production Rates Next Pd. 1000 units	This Pd. 1000 units	Asm. Labor $ per unit	Asm. # Men Assigned	# Men Hired Or Fired (–)		Asm. Overtime # Hours		
									10

143

Industry _____ Corporation _____ Div. –Plt. _____ Period _____ Section _____

PRODUCT 1

Price Next Period $ per unit	Advertising Budget $1000	Promotion Budget $1000	Prod. Dev. Budget $1000	Mkt. Res. Budget $1000	MR– Price ¢ PU	MR– Adv. $1000	MR– Qual. ¢ PU	MR– P.D. $1000	
									2

Raw Mat'l $ per unit	Fab. Production Rates Next Pd. 1000 units	This Pd. 1000 units	Fab. Labor $ per unit	Fab. # Men Assigned	# Men Hired Or Fired (–)	Fab. Overtime # Hours	
							3

Purchased Parts $ per unit	Asm. Production Rates Next Pd. 1000 units	This Pd. 1000 units	Asm. Labor $ per unit	Asm. # Men Assigned	# Men Hired Or Fired (–)	Asm. Overtime # Hours	
							4

PRODUCT 2

Price Next Period $ per unit	Advertising Budget $1000	Promotion Budget $1000	Prod. Dev. Budget $1000	Mkt. Res. Budget $1000	MR– Price ¢ PU	MR– Adv. $1000	MR– Qual. ¢ PU	MR– P.D. $1000	
									5

Raw Mat'l $ per unit	Fab. Production Rates Next Pd. 1000 units	This Pd. 1000 units	Fab. Labor $ per unit	Fab. # Men Assigned	# Men Hired Or Fired (–)	Fab. Overtime # Hours	
							6

Purchased Parts $ per units	Asm. Production Rates Next Pd. 1000 units	This Pd. 1000 units	Asm. Labor $ per unit	Asm. # Men Assigned	# Men Hired Or Fired (–)	Asm. Overtime # Hours	
							7

PRODUCT 3

Price Next Period $ per unit	Advertising Budget $1000	Promotion Budget $1000	Prod. Dev. Budget $1000	Mkt. Res. Budget $1000	MR– Price ¢ PU	MR– Adv. $1000	MR– Qual. ¢ PU	MR– P.D. $1000	
									8

Raw Mat'l $ per unit	Fab. Production Rates Next Pd. 1000 units	This Pd. 1000 units	Fab. Labor $ per unit	Fab # Men Assigned	# Men Hired Or Fired (–)	Fab. Overtime # Hours	
							9

Purchased Parts $ per unit	Asm. Production Rates Next Pd. 1000 units	This Pd. 1000 units	Asm. Labor $ per unit	Asm. # Men Assigned	# Men Hired Or Fired (–)	Asm. Overtime # Hours	
							10

Industry _____ Corporation _____ Div. –Plt. _____ Period _____ Section _____

PRODUCT 1

Price Next Period $ per unit	Advertising Budget $1000	Promotion Budget $1000	Prod. Dev. Budget $1000	Mkt. Res. Budget $1000	MR– Price ¢ PU	MR– Adv. $1000	MR– Qual. ¢ PU	MR– P.D. $1000	
									2

Raw Mat'l $ per unit	Fab. Production Rates Next Pd. 1000 units	This Pd. 1000 units	Fab. Labor $ per unit	Fab. # Men Assigned	# Men Hired Or Fired (–)	Fab. Overtime # Hours	
							3

Purchased Parts $ per unit	Asm. Production Rates Next Pd. 1000 units	This Pd. 1000 units	Asm. Labor $ per unit	Asm. # Men Assigned	# Men Hired Or Fired (–)	Asm. Overtime # Hours	
							4

PRODUCT 2

Price Next Period $ per unit	Advertising Budget $1000	Promotion Budget $1000	Prod. Dev. Budget $1000	Mkt. Res. Budget $1000	MR– Price ¢ PU	MR– Adv. $1000	MR– Qual. ¢ PU	MR– P.D. $1000	
									5

Raw Mat'l $ per unit	Fab. Production Rates Next Pd. 1000 units	This Pd. 1000 units	Fab. Labor $ per unit	Fab. # Men Assigned	# Men Hired Or Fired (–)	Fab. Overtime # Hours	
							6

Purchased Parts $ per units	Asm. Production Rates Next Pd. 1000 units	This Pd. 1000 units	Asm. Labor $ per unit	Asm. # Men Assigned	# Men Hired Or Fired (–)	Asm. Overtime # Hours	
							7

PRODUCT 3

Price Next Period $ per unit	Advertising Budget $1000	Promotion Budget $1000	Prod. Dev. Budget $1000	Mkt. Res. Budget $1000	MR– Price ¢ PU	MR– Adv. $1000	MR– Qual. ¢ PU	MR– P.D. $1000	
									8

Raw Mat'l $ per unit	Fab. Production Rates Next Pd. 1000 units	This Pd. 1000 units	Fab. Labor $ per unit	Fab # Men Assigned	# Men Hired Or Fired (–)	Fab. Overtime # Hours	
							9

Purchased Parts $ per unit	Asm. Production Rates Next Pd. 1000 units	This Pd. 1000 units	Asm. Labor $ per unit	Asm. # Men Assigned	# Men Hired Or Fired (–)	Asm. Overtime # Hours	
							10

MANAGEMENT SIMULATION – CORPORATE DECISION FORM

Corporation _____   Period _____   Section _____

External Financial Decisions

Purchase Securities ($1000)	Dividends ($1000)	90-Day Loans ($1000)	One Year Loans ($1000)	Five Year Notes ($1000)	Sell Stock ($1000)

Forecasted Earnings Per Share

This Period	Next Period	Two Periods in Future	Three Periods in Future	

Building and Equipment Purchases

Division 1		Division 2		Division 3	
Northern Plant ($1000)	Southern Plant ($1000)	Northern Plant ($1000)	Southern Plant ($1000)	Northern Plant ($1000)	Southern Plant ($1000)

Cash Transfers to and from Divisions

Division 1	Division 2	Division 3	

Product Transfers Between Plants

	Plant from			No. of Units (1000)	Plant to			Unit Price
	Product	Plant	Industry		Product	Plant	Industry	
1.								
2.								
3.								
4.								
5.								

149

MANAGEMENT SIMULATION — CORPORATE DECISION FORM

Corporation _____ Period _____ Section _____

External Financial Decisions

Purchase Securities ($1000)	Dividends ($1000)	90-Day Loans ($1000)	One Year Loans ($1000)	Five Year Notes ($1000)	Sell Stock ($1000)

Forecasted Earnings Per Share

This Period	Next Period	Two Periods in Future	Three Periods in Future	

Building and Equipment Purchases

Division 1		Division 2		Division 3	
Northern Plant ($1000)	Southern Plant ($1000)	Northern Plant ($1000)	Southern Plant ($1000)	Northern Plant ($1000)	Southern Plant ($1000)

Cash Transfers to and from Divisions

Division 1	Division 2	Division 3	

Product Transfers Between Plants

	Plant from			No. of Units (1000)	Plant to			Unit Price
	Product	Plant	Industry		Product	Plant	Industry	
1.								
2.								
3.								
4.								
5.								

MANAGEMENT SIMULATION — CORPORATE DECISION FORM

Corporation _____   Period _____   Section _____

External Financial Decisions

Purchase Securities ($1000)	Dividends ($1000)	90-Day Loans ($1000)	One Year Loans ($1000)	Five Year Notes ($1000)	Sell Stock ($1000)

Forecasted Earnings Per Share

This Period	Next Period	Two Periods in Future	Three Periods in Future	

Building and Equipment Purchases

Division 1		Division 2		Division 3	
Northern Plant ($1000)	Southern Plant ($1000)	Northern Plant ($1000)	Southern Plant ($1000)	Northern Plant ($1000)	Southern Plant ($1000)

Cash Transfers to and from Divisions

Division 1	Division 2	Division 3	

Product Transfers Between Plants

	Plant from			No. of Units (1000)	Plant to			Unit Price
	Product	Plant	Industry		Product	Plant	Industry	
1.								
2.								
3.								
4.								
5.								

153